InterMedia in South Asia

The emergence of new media today in South Asia has signalled an event, the meaning of which remains obscure but whose reality is rapidly evolving along gradients of intensity and experience. Contemporary media in and from South Asia have come to sense a new arrangement of value, sensation, and force – new forms of becoming that might be usefully termed as 'media ecologies'. This evolution from nation-based forms of communication (Doordarshan, All India Radio, the 'national' feudal romance) to simultaneous global ones conform and mutate the structures of feeling of local, national, diasporic and transnational belonging. This collection of original essays is concerned with understanding how people are making meaning from new media and how subaltern tinkering (pirating, peer-to-peer file sharing, hacking, noise jamming, indymedia, etc.) does things to and in new media. This exciting works helps us to make sense of the creation of new publics, new affects and new experiences of pleasure and value in convergences of intermedia in a fast developing South Asia context.

This book was originally published as a special issue of *South Asian Popular Culture*.

Rajinder Dudrah is Senior Lecturer and Director of the Centre for Screen Studies at the University of Manchester, UK. He has researched and published widely in film, media and cultural studies in international journals. His books include *Bollywood: Sociology Goes to the Movies* (2006), *Bhangra: Birmingham and Beyond* (2007), *The Bollywood Reader* (2008), and *Theorising World Cinema* (2011).

Sangita Gopal is an Associate Professor of English and Cinema Studies at the University of Oregon, USA. She has researched and published in the fields of postcolonial studies, film studies and feminist theory. Her publications include an edited volume of essays, *Global Bollywood: Travels of Hindi Film Music* (2008) and *Conjugations: Family and Film Form in New Bollywood Cinema* (2011). She is currently working on a project entitled *Mutant Media* that looks at issues of intermediality and time in a postcolonial context.

Amit S. Rai is Senior Lecturer in New Media and Communication at Queen Mary, University of London, UK. He has published across the range of queer, feminist, postcolonial, and media studies, increasingly focusing on questions of affect, sensation, technology, and political economy. He is the author of *Untimely Bollywood: Globalization and India's New Media Assemblage* (2009). He is currently at work on a study of Indian mobile phone media and its emergent ecology of sensation.

Anustup Basu is Associate Professor in English and Cinema Studies at the University of Illinois, USA, at Urbana-Champaign. His essays on cinema, new media, and philosophy/politics of information have appeared in various international journals. He is the author of *Bollywood in the Age of New Media: The Geo-televisual Aesthetic* (2010).

InterMedia in South Asia
The Fourth Screen

Edited by
**Rajinder Dudrah, Sangita Gopal,
Amit S. Rai and Anustup Basu**

LONDON AND NEW YORK

First published 2012
by Routledge
2 Park Square, Milton Park, Abingdon, Oxon, OX14 4RN

Simultaneously published in the USA and Canada
by Routledge
711 Third Avenue, New York, NY 10017

First issued in paperback 2017

Routledge is an imprint of the Taylor & Francis Group, an informa business

© 2012 Taylor & Francis

This book is a reproduction of *South Asian Popular Culture,* volume 8, issue 2. The Publisher requests to those authors who may be citing this book to state, also, the bibliographical details of the special issue on which the book was based.

All rights reserved. No part of this book may be reprinted or reproduced or utilised in any form or by any electronic, mechanical, or other means, now known or hereafter invented, including photocopying and recording, or in any information storage or retrieval system, without permission in writing from the publishers.

Trademark notice: Product or corporate names may be trademarks or registered trademarks, and are used only for identification and explanation without intent to infringe.

British Library Cataloguing in Publication Data
A catalogue record for this book is available from the British Library

Typeset in Times New Roman
by Saxon Graphics Ltd, Derby

Publisher's Note
The publisher would like to make readers aware that the chapters in this book may be referred to as articles as they are identical to the articles published in the special issue. The publisher accepts responsibility for any inconsistencies that may have arisen in the course of preparing this volume for print.

ISBN 13: 978-1-138-11079-3 (pbk)
ISBN 13: 978-0-415-69818-4 (hbk)

Contents

1. Intermedia emergence: The fourth screen
   Rajinder Dudrah, Sangita Gopal, Amit Rai and Anustup Basu   1

2. Desktop deities: Hindu temples, online cultures and
   the politics of remediation
   Madhavi Mallapragada   6

3. Some annotations on the film festival as an emerging medium in India
   Pooja Rangan   19

4. Confessions of the (ethnic) narcissist: Intermedia in diaspora
   Ani Maitra   38

5. Zee TV: Diasporic non-terrestrial television in Europe
   Rajinder Dudrah   58

6. 'Beaming it live': 24-hour television news, the spectator and
   the spectacle of the 2002 Gujarat carnage
   Anuja Jain   70

7. Muslim punks online: A diasporic Pakistani music subculture
   on the Internet
   Dhiraj Murthy   87

8. 'Through A Lens Starkly': An exploration of JU Medialab's
   National Instruments Project archive
   Anustup Basu   101

9. Composite photography
   Amit Rai   111

   Index   119

Intermedia emergence: The fourth screen

Rajinder Dudrah, Sangita Gopal, Amit Rai and Anustup Basu

We live today, in the Diaspora, and on the subcontinent enwrapped in increasingly instantaneous media flows. Yet this is not a more complex media ecology than that which prior generations experienced. It is qualitatively different, and its conceptual framework must also qualitatively change. Not surprisingly, many critics have noted how globalization is marked by intensive media becomings: rates of flow, density of information, gradients of noise (entropy) in communication channels, emergent media-body multiplicities, resonation of intensity across populations. In places as disparate as Jackson Heights (Queens, NY), Star City (Birmingham, UK), Jahangirabad, Bhopal (Madhya Pradesh), Chor Bazaar, Mumbai (Maharashtra), or Maruthahalli (Bangalore), changes in access to technology, and shifts in computer-aided perception have transformed the very nature of value, consumption, pleasure, and work. Capitalist, non-capitalist, bazaar-capitalist – new media today moves and exists across technological platforms to valorize brands and logos, styles and sensation, movements and affects in a way that necessitates a clear consideration of the relevance and limitation of nation-based analyses of these becomings. The movement of information is better understood not as the free play of virtual and arbitrary signifiers disseminating the order words of the secular, modernizing nation-state, but through concepts such as patterned flow, gradients of intensity, molar and minor becomings, controlled modulation, affective and emergent capacities, bodily kinesthesia, and creative value. These concepts, taken from a range of contemporary forms of critique – feminist, Marxist, postcolonial, biopolitical – necessitate that we go back to older critical frameworks with a pragmatic understanding of their changing domain of validity.

The emergence of the new media today in South Asia has signaled an event the meaning of which remains obscure, but whose reality is rapidly evolving along gradients of intensity. These phase transitions are the occasion when fluctuations (noise) in a volatile system (a body, a media ecology, a public sphere) have both macroscopic effects, and a new capacity to 'sense' shifts in force. Contemporary media ecologies in and from South Asia have come to sense a new arrangement of value, sensation, and force. This evolution from nation-based forms of communication (Doordarshan, All India Radio, the 'national' feudal romance) conforms and mutates the structure of feeling of national and local belonging. We, as scholars of South Asian popular culture, are as concerned with understanding how people are making meaning from the new media as how subaltern tinkering (pirating, peer-to-peer file sharing, hacking, noise jamming, 'Indymedia,' etc.) does things to and in the new media. Meaning and pragmatics, therefore, are feedback looped together in the creation of new publics, new affects, and new experiences of pleasure and value.

Consider, for instance, this recent précis of the emergence of value-added services (VAS) in India's booming mobile phone market. The company making these prognostications is Delhi-based one-97.

> From one page newspapers and theatre to ... silent movies to ... television to ... cable to ... internet content on ones [sic] fingertips the media has gone through a rapid evolution. We talk about the shrinking global village but the true potential of media and its reach is yet to be unleashed. We have barely scratched the surface of [the] Fourth screen – The Mobile (for the uninitiated the first three screens are Silver screen, TV screen and Computer screen), it is

perhaps the most ubiquitous of screens in our lives today. Going by the mobile penetration level India is perfectly poised to leapfrog the internet revolution to land directly into the mobile broadband revolution. It has already begun with the fast changes on all fronts of digital media including improvement in handset features, network bandwidth and quality & variety of content. Mobile has fast evolved from just being a device to talk to a centerpiece of our lives. Traditionally, VAS business in the country has been driven by the ABC genres which are Astrology, Bollywood and Cricket. The first wave of applications was focused on ABC since the consumers were exploring mobile as a medium and were getting used to it. In the first wave of mobile VAS, service providers could get away with sending the same content to the large and varied Indian population e.g. Bollywood content to every user whether he is in Tamil Nadu, Gujarat or Bihar or Delhi. However users are now looking for varieties of content tailored to suit their individual tastes. All in all there is business in addressing the long tail of customers also. Through this feature we will try to look at the evolution of the mobile content business in India and explore the way forward. Needless to say it's still early days for the mobile content business and we are in an evolutionary stage as far as business models are concerned. So all questions and thoughts are welcome! (one-97)

What are the trajectories and tendencies of this evolution? Perhaps the central question from the perspective of companies like one-97 is how to create value from the flow of information. What are the forces with which such a company contends? What type of innovation and branding govern in this media ecology? From the perspective of the differentially subaltern user, the central question is how to make this thing (in this case a cell phone) work to its full potential given a changing set of needs, capacities (financial, bodily, attitudinal, cognitive, etc.), and temporal limits. These two questions are not opposed to each other (as in a classical antinomy), but form a permeable interface across which two regimes of value self organize. Intermedia ecologies have both equilibriums and unstable states, and noise in one system becomes the occasion of a critical threshold in another; a negligible control parameter (force) in one system, is sensed by another. These are emergent ecologies, with capacities and structurations for which there is no map, only a diagram of becoming.

One regime is centered on the residual and emergent order words of a rapidly liberalizing socialist state: global village, Fourth screen, transparency, individual tastes, value-added, multicultural content, entrepreneurial business models (as Foucault reminds us in the Birth of Biopolitics, neoliberalism is first and foremost an entrepreneurism of the self). The other regime, submerged in the interstices of this ordered grid of value added, correlates the flow of information with heterogeneous intensive flows and improvizational pragmatics. These flows are pre-individual in the sense that their dynamics are both populational and passionate. Thus, we can say that critical diagrams of global media production and consumption chart intensive flows as desiring machines that both grid desire and potentialize it.

This is where South Asian media finds itself today. Surrounded by and, partly, in symbiosis with a US-led occupational force that has 'embedded' certain flows of strategic and policy information around the military operations in Afghanistan and Pakistan, India is riding the murderous tiger of American decline. Hybridizing neoliberalism is not the same as deterritorializing it because the first is still dialectically identitarian (conceptual), while the latter is ontologically intensive (physio-chemical). Therefore, if the cultural practices of contemporary consumerism – represented by the KJo (Karan Johar) brand of filmmaking – seem to hybridize neoliberalism and monumentalize Nehruvian state socialism, we should be wary of claims that proclaim such hybridity as resistance.

Our gaze is directed toward those untimely practices that are directed at the durations of the body, an embodied ontology of duration – contractions and expansions of perception-attention, variable rates of intensive rhythms, bundling and unfolding embedded populations of processes. It is at this stratum of molecular, mnemonic, bacteriological, biopolitical life that media technologies must be diagrammed, and representations situated.

The essays in this issue provide us with useful lenses to look at some of the ways in which these micro-punctual, non-linear flows take place, in a globalizing 'South Asian' theater taken virtually. In her discussion about film festivals in India, Pooja Rangan poses incisive questions about how such cultural phenomena are to be theorized in a new media ecology, in which state sponsored, axiomatic monitoring of culture is no longer tenable and the 'black box' of cinema in itself has been exploded. She invokes Bruno Latour's actor-network theory (ANT) and problematizes it, along with traditional, older methods of discerning ideological scripts inherent in specific or general instances of festival programming. Rangan's call, among other things, is thus for a complex critical model that would be able to account for 'new relations to space and time' produced by the 'specific scale, seriality, and intensities of festival programming.'

Through a critical engagement with anthropologist and filmmaker Harjant Singh's partly autobiographical video essay 'Milind Soman Made Me Gay', Ani Maitra attempts to complicate Ray Chow's notion of 'coercive mimeticism' by which the ethnic figure is interpolated into a schema of circuitous narcissism that summon her to incessantly mimic her own ethnicity. It is, however, a transindividual narcissism, mediating the ground between the ethnic artist and the community. Unlike Chow's skeptical take, Maitra wonders whether this zone of in-between-ness can actually harbor transformative potential and throw up dissonant performances of identity in an overall, globally fluctuating dispensation of 'diaspora, narcissism, and intermedia.'

Rajinder Dudrah's essay introduces and analyzes the Zee TV channel through a framework of textual analysis that pays attention to its emergence amidst an historical overview of minority ethnic representation in the Western European media. His essay draws on qualitative interviews undertaken in the city of Birmingham (UK) with Zee TV viewers, and focuses on two of the channel's programmes – *Your Zindagi* and *Euro Zindagi*. Dudrah convincingly argues that both programmes aim to simultaneously address and construct its UK and wider European diasporic South Asian audiences. In conclusion, he offers an assessment of the development of the channel's increasing popularity amidst the deregulation and liberalization of the international audio and visual spheres, and amidst Zee TV's possibilities in engaging with a number of different emerging socio-cultural and political identities, both progressive and otherwise.

In a remarkably ambitious essay, Anuja Jain visits the 24/7 television phenomenon of Godhra (2002) in order to understand how a torrid 'informatization' of the event resulted in a disjunction 'between the present and the archive of the past.' She meticulously reconstructs a scenario in which a pervasive ideology of 'ubiquity, liveness, (and) instantaneity' informs television reportage primed for the newly emergent, globally aspiring middle class consumer-spectator and reduces the event into a crisis of overstimulation and exhaustion. She persuasively calls out attention to a new kinetic ecology of language in the tripartite interface of politics, technology and the market. A sober evaluation of the effects of this environment, its sublimation of perhaps a new majoritarian common sense calls for a rethinking of hardened categories like citizenship, communalism, secularism, and national identity.

In an insightful essay, Madhavi Mallapragada examines a new age assemblage between Hindu ritualism, ontologies of presence and sacredness, and digital capitalism, transnationalism, and new media consumption. She critically engages with Bolter and Grusin's notion of remediation to demonstrate how, in what she calls 'desktop deity cultures,' older media of Hindu public religiosity like photographs, calendar art, the analog sacred texts and temple books, and audio tapes of religious discourse mediate and in turn are remediated by contemporary processes of virtualization and connectivity. Mallapragada's work invites us to rethink ideas of embodiment, presence, and materiality in relation to traditional practices like Darshan.

Dhiraj Murthy's fascinating essay demonstrates, from another angle, how viral spreads and flows between transnational spaces can build up progressive energies that affirm identities against statist-informatic 'profiles' and at the same time make those identities themselves dynamic. Using an ethnographic model that is partly based on face-to-face interviews and partly immersed in the very sphere of virtuality and kinesis that he is studying, Murthy looks into a transnational Islamic punk rock scenario that asserts itself in the face of post 9/11 and 7/7 Islamophobia. Using 'Taqwacore,' a particular scene like that as a case study, Murthy shows us how, in the age of Flickr albums, YouTube videos, MySpace pages, Facebook pages, BitTorrent and other peer-to-peer formats, online exchanges in a virtual diaspora transform and shape offline globalizing cultures.

Anustup Basu's essay explores a remarkable multi-media archive (short films, still photographs, photo animations, sound installations), on the closed down public sector unit National Instruments Ltd., built by members and affiliates of Jadavpur University's media lab. Critically reading the myriad, evocative sounds and pictures of an abandoned factory site that is, as if, sealed off in a bubble of time, Basu considers the status of such an archive in our informational age. What pathways and forkings of memory and affect do these myriad visuals and echoes (of dead telephones, ghostly machines, abandoned love letters, or a shirt hung up to dry for an eternity) yield? Do they tell us some 'truth' about the factory and its workers? Are they supposed to represent something? What aesthetic and political questions about the ontology of the image can be raised through such sights and sounds in what is, reportedly, the age of the postmodern?

Amit Rai's short, but illuminating, photo essay strongly underlines the core purpose of this special issue: to bring thinking out of boxed pieties of Renaissance perspectivalism, representation, or reflection theory. It is to discern the birth of the image as a procedure of ecogenesis. In this the awry energies of a multiplicity are not enframed, captured, and consigned to death, but the image itself is a durational tracing of lines of flight between, say, Bollywood and graphic novels in the back of a rickshaw, or even possibly, if the urban archive of multiplicities and sensations were to be so extended, the old avant-garde dream of meeting the umbrella and the sewing machine at a realm beyond mere representation. Rai's meditative commentary is on how one can see the images as events that exceed their actualization. They are mutating, not enframing devices; they solicit our 'perceptual capacities away from equilibrium.'

That the city has now become the screen is sort of a cliché of our times. However, this paradoxical thought image that imposes a flat two dimensional surface onto a lived three dimensional space can be better understood if one realizes that the long gestating promise of our media revolution has been precisely to break the screen itself as the final barrier. The screen-city coupling is thus a shocking dispersal of multiplicities; it is an ecology of sensations that increasingly operate over and beyond vertical instruments of policing and priestly mediations of the paternal state. To think culture, value, affect, ideology, and politics in this scenario is perhaps to think beyond linear assurances of an Althusserian model of interpellation and the overall integrated ideas of the subject, unity, and the law. In different ways, the essays in this volume brilliantly advance in that direction.

References

Foucault, Michel. *The Birth of Biopolitics: Lectures at the College de France*. Basingstoke: Palgrave Macmillan, 2008. Print.

one-97. afaqs! *The complete Indian advertising, media & marketing site*. n.d. Web. 15 Jul. 2009. http://www.afaqs.com/main1.html

Desktop deities: Hindu temples, online cultures and the politics of remediation

Madhavi Mallapragada

Department of Radio-Television-Film, University of Texas, Austin, USA

> This study examines Hindu temples on the Web by focusing on three key types, the temple homepage, the commercial puja site and the Hindu discourse site. It argues that Hindu temples sites demonstrate the emergence of what I call 'desktop deity culture,' constituted through the practices of digital darshan, online rituals and virtual Hinduism. These Web practices in turn exemplify the 'remediation' (Bolter and Grusin) of new media conceptualizations of digitality, network capital flows, hypertextuality and virtuality as they are articulated to ideas of the Hindu image, embodied ritual practice and the temporal and spatial logic of the temple as sacred place. Remediation in Bolter and Grusin's influential theorization of new media is a refashioning characterized by a 'double logic' whereby new media 'remediate and are remediated by their predecessors' (55). Hindu temple sites, I argue, are repurposing 'older' media forms such as photographs of deities, Hindu calendar art, the analog sacred texts and temple books, audio tapes of religious discourse through their textual and discursive practices of representing online temples. Likewise, aspects of digital media such as hypertextual connectivity, virtual forms of dis/embodiment and im/materiality and mobile flows of capital and culture are deployed to pay service to place-centric, embodied and material practices shaping Hindu temple cultures. In this remediation of Hindu representational forms and material practices with new media ideologies and practices, both Hindu temples and new media as cultural forms are reinvented as 'desktop deity cultures.'

Introduction

In December 1996, *Time*'s cover story, 'Finding God on the Web' focusing on the explosion of religious activity online, noted that 'the marriage of God and computer networks' was yet another chapter in a long-standing alliance between religion and cutting-edge communications technologies. Nonetheless, the writers wondered: 'Will the Net change religion? Is it possible, that God, in a networked age, will look, somehow different?' (Ramo and Burke). Scholarly research on religion and new media has extended such questions to examine how traditional ideas of ritual worship, sacred space and community interact with the virtualization of religion. Stephen O'Leary (781–808), Christopher Helland ('Surfing'; 'Religion Online'; 'Online Religion'), Lorne Dawson and Douglas Cowan (*Religion Online*), Brenda Brasher (*Give me that Online Religion*), Heidi Campbell (*Exploring*), and Stephen Jacobs (1103–1121) among others, have highlighted the diverse nature of religious sites and the heteregenous practices that constitute religious activity online. Their research is significant for examining issues such as the reconstruction of hypertextual space as sacred space, the reorientation of ritual in an online setting, the negotiation of 'embodied' religious experience on the Web and the change in dominant understandings of religious community in light of the prolific growth in online faith, spirituality and religion-based networks.

While cyberspace may be, in the words of Brenda Brasher, 'the unexpectedly novel terrain of human spirituality' (5), it is being increasingly mobilized for traditional as well as alternative expressions of faith, spirituality and religion. Computer-generated sacred imagery, audio and video streams of prayers, e-rituals and Web-based faith communities demonstrate some of the features of online religion. From a new media cultural studies perspective, the incorporation and appropriation of digital technologies to advance, reinforce and, arguably, transform the domain of religion presents a fascinating context to explore and complicate conceptualizations of virtual time-space, interactivity, digitality and online community formations. As analog religious signifiers get digitized and uploaded, cyber rituals and pilgrimages engender virtual sensoriums of worship and the network facilitates collective imaginings of faith, ideas of sacred space and time become critical to our understanding of the spatial-temporal dimensions of the contemporary Web. Recalling Stephen O'Leary's point that 'the fundamental problem of religious communication is how best to represent and mediate the sacred' (787), it is productive to ask: How does the Web engage with ideas of sacred space and time? How are the spatial-temporal elements constitutive of the 'sacred' mediated in a virtual environment? How do new media formulations of time-space interact with religious notions of divine time (or timelessness) and the virtual nature of faith? What then, are the politics of new media practices in shaping what Stephen Jacobs (1103–1121) titles the 'virtually sacred'?

Examining the intersections between traditional and emergent online constructions of the sacred complicate our understanding of digital media cultures by revealing how the 'new' often includes an innovative recasting of 'older' mediations of the sacred. Religious websites also signal the repurposing of existing structures and institutions to stay relevant in the age of digital capitalism, transnationalism and new media consumption. Virtually accessible at all times, religious websites are actively shaping a consumptive culture whereby patrons at their convenience enter a site not only to pray, share and reflect, but also to search, download, and shop for products in its spiritual mall. In this context, examining the practices of online religion also allow us to critically engage with the discursive category of 'new' media.

This article contributes to the literature on religion and new media by focusing on Hindu temple cultures on the Web. Using four sites, Hindutempleofatlanta.org (henceforth HTA.org), Saranam.com, Eprarthana.com and Vmandir.com as prime examples, it discusses new media iterations of sacred space, ritual worship and the temple-centric experience in the Hindu tradition. Analytically speaking, three 'types' constitute the domain of Hindu temples on the Web: (1) the temple homepage, which functions as the online home for a physical temple; (2) the commercial puja site, which facilitates rituals services in prominent temples on behalf of their clients for a fee; and (3) the Hindu discourse site, which presents the temple as a virtual space for mediation, prayer and explication of Hindu religious discourse. As the virtual home of The Hindu Temple of Atlanta, in Riverdale, Georgia, HTA.org exemplifies the first type of site; Saranam.com and Eprarthana.com in the business of facilitating rituals in India's famous temples exemplify the second, while Vmandir.com, a virtual temple or mandir, exemplifies the third type. Such an analytical distinction aside, several site features overlap across the above-mentioned three types; for example, HTA.org facilitates online commercial transactions for ritual services conducted on its temple premises while Saranam.com provides its customers, shopping for ritual, with detailed explication of the Hindu myths and traditions attached to its products.

This analysis foregrounds the key online practices of Hindu temple sites and engages with their politics of representing sacred time-space, virtualized forms of ritual and contemporary modes of Hindu religiosity. It is centrally concerned with the following questions: What online practices shape the emergent domain of Hindu temple sites? How do websites engage with the notion of sacred time-space? Since in the Hindu tradition, the temple as well as images of anthropomorphic deities, symbols, and saints are constitutive of the sacred (Eck), how do websites articulate ideologies of place, physical architecture and embodied rituals to the temples' new media contexts? Likewise, does new media virtuality function strategically to foreground the 'virtual' nature of belief and faith that in turn transforms a material, physical order into an immaterial, sacred one? How are new media technologies and communications being articulated to Hindu ritual and temple cultures?

The central argument is that Hindu temples sites demonstrate the emergence of what I call 'desktop deity culture' constituted through the practices of digital darshan, online rituals and virtual Hinduism. These Web practices in turn exemplify the 'remediation' (Bolter and Grusin) of new media conceptualizations of digitality, network capital flows, hypertextuality and virtuality as they are articulated to ideas of the Hindu image, embodied ritual practice and the temporal and spatial logic of the temple as sacred place. Remediation in Bolter and Grusin's influential theorization of new media is a refashioning characterized by a 'double logic' whereby new media 'remediate and are remediated by their predecessors' (55). Hindu temple sites, I argue, are repurposing 'older' media forms such as photographs of deities, Hindu calendar art, the analog sacred texts and temple books, audio tapes of religious discourse through their textual and discursive practices of representing online temples. Likewise, aspects of digital media such as hypertextual connectivity, virtual forms of dis/embodiment and im/materiality and mobile flows of capital and culture are deployed to pay service to place-centric, embodied and material practices shaping Hindu temple cultures. In this remediation of Hindu representational forms and material practices with new media ideologies and practices, both Hindu temples and new media as cultural forms are reinvented as 'desktop deity cultures.'

In the next section, I offer a brief overview of HTA.org, Saranam.com, E-prarthana.com and vmandir.com and highlight key textual and institutional features that shape the virtualization of Hindu temple culture. The final section elaborates on the idea of 'desktop deity cultures' by exploring the contours of its three key practices – digital darshan, online rituals and virtual Hinduism.

I. "The divine link"[1]*: Reconfiguring the Hindu temple on the Web*

At Iowa State University's virtual Hindu temple, students use head-mounted displays and other virtual reality technologies to enter an immersive environment based on a sixteenth-century Hindu temple located in India.[2] A collaborative project between the Virtual Reality Applications Center and the Department of Philosophy and Religious Studies, this technological experiment in recreating the sensorial complexity of the temple-going experience, marks an exception in the domain of Hindu temples on the Web. The latter's digital turn, for the most part, has been in the direction of hyptertextual links, digitized imagery, online discourse, ritual-centric e-commerce and temple homepages.

HTA.org, the homepage of the Hindu Temple of Atlanta, represents a prolific category – the temple homepage. It exemplifies a growing trend among prominent temple institutions in India, the US and elsewhere, strategically to deploy the Web for maintaining, extending and, arguably, transforming the presence and relevance of temple cultures in the lives of an increasingly mobile, networked, transnational Hindu base. The site also highlights the shifting boundaries of the 'temple' as physical locations are negotiated with virtual homes; often, such negotiations involve making some services of the temple network-accessible while simultaneously privileging the temple's physical identity. This is exemplified on HTA.org through the juxtapositioning of digital photographs of the temple complex, its deities, priests and ritual scenes with hyperlinks to online registration for pujas, Balavihar (Sunday school) and volunteering. As activities that are structured within the time-space routines of the physical temple – pujas, Balavihar and volunteering – notwithstanding the online access to them, they point to the continuing relevance of the physically bounded sacred structure to the temple's identity. Similarly, by visually foregrounding the constitutive elements of the Hindu sacred (Eck 32–58), namely the abode of the divine (temple structure) the mediator of devotee-divine interactions (priest), the embodied signifier of divine presence (deities) and the sacralizing of time-space (rituals), HTA.org reminds the online devotee of the centrality of the temple to the apprehensions of the sacred. The homepage here serves a common function of temple sites wherein network-space facilitates a greater investment in the place-centric activities of the temple. Nevertheless, by giving its patrons the flexibility of going to its virtual instead of its physical home to get information, seek out services and commit time and money, the Hindu Temple of Atlanta signals new patterns being established in the communication and organizational practices of a traditional institution.

In this context, photographs play a prominent role in narrativizing the temple. For example, in the 'History' section, images spanning a decade visually reconstruct specific events as defining moments in the literal and symbolic emergence of the temple.[3] Images of the land grading, the ground-breaking ceremony, sculptors (from India) at work on the temple architecture, and the rituals of idol consecration among others, frame a larger narrative about the temple's history wherein the Hindu Indian community's cultural pride, devotion to authenticity and spiritual resilience in the wake of institutional challenges emerge as key motifs. The 'photo gallery' shifts the emphasis from the temple's past to its present by visually presenting scenes of everyday worship at the temple and including images of deities, ritual offerings (fruit, flowers, lamp), temple priests and devotees. Taking it's cue from HTA.org where the @ symbol is invoked to indicate divine presence ('Balaji@HTA' alongside a photograph of the deity Balaji's idol), it is argued here that the digitized online photograph plays a prominent role in mediating the network user's perspective on the temple's past and present. Stated differently, it is the homepage, with its strategic visual iconography, where the institutional challenges of the temple are inscribed; its 'Indian' architectural style authenticated; and where the community's memories are uploaded. With a digital archive of its past and a virtual representation of its sacred space, HTA.org, the homepage, is where the temple, to use the new media colloquialism, is @.

India-based Saranam.com and Eprarthana.com exemplify the harnessing of Hindu ritual, virtual identities and mobile cultures to generate new economies of faith and capital. As commercial puja sites, both specialize in conducting puja (ritual worship) services in several of India's prominent temples on behalf of the devotee for a fee. In the Hinduism, both home and temple pujas are significant; however, the hegemonic orthodox, Vedic tradition has historically privileged both elaborate forms of public rituals (in temples) as well the Brahmin male's priestly mediations of the human-divine interactions (Wadley 121–22). Like the temple priest who typically customizes the puja according to deity, occasion and astrological data, Saranam.com lets its customers generate their puja orders by selecting from a drop-down menu of temples, deities, rituals and puja dates. Customers can further personalize the order by requesting that additional information such as names or astrological details be included into the puja service. Once the order is made, Saranam.com's local representative visits the destination temple and ensures that the puja is conducted on behalf of the online devotee; the latter subsequently receives the temple receipt and the prasad (ritual offerings signifying divine blessings) in the mail (Taparia M15; Sink 6).

Mobilized around the puja service are Saranam.com's three secondary services of astrology, shopping and information guide. Featuring live chat, personal astrologers and horoscope-matching, Saranam.com packages its commercial astrological services as human and not computer-generated.[4] While fairly limited in its product offerings (puja bells, lamps, Rudrakshas/rosaries), its online store imagines its clientele as globally dispersed, evidenced in the rendering of pricing information in ten different currencies. As a guide to Hindu temples, Saranam.com breaks down the vastly complex domain of Hindu deities, ritual traditions, mythology, and occasion-specific puja services into a series of browsable categories; the category 'Ganesh Temples', for example, leads to a Ganesh-specific myth and information page with links to prominent Ganesh temples in India that are part of Saranam's electronic network. Each temple link in turn provides a brief temple history and an online order form and shopping cart for pujas.[5]

Saranam.com's key competitor in the Hindu marketplace, Eprarthana.com, is comparable to the former in terms of the key services it provides. However, with its Google-powered search box (to sift through the 2000-plus temples in its network), prominently featured advertisements for Vedic astrology, Hindu art and sculptures, as well as its promotional strategies such as 'Deity of the Day' (akin to the 'what's hot' feature on shopping sites), Eprarthana.com is the more conspicuously commercially-driven of the two. Eprarthana.com is also distinct in that it features 'virtual pujas' where users, to the accompaniment of sacred hymns, perform online ritual worship to specific deities by clicking on puja offerings such as flowers, fruit and incense.

At a broader level, the virtualization of pujas through sites like Saranam.com point to a reworking of an existing Hindu tradition where conducting rituals and worship on behalf of another is sanctioned. Further, Eprarthana.com's ritual worship through digitized flowers, incense, and online prayers foregrounds an underlying tension between phenomenological and virtual apprehensions of the Hindu sacred. As Diana L. Eck notes, even as idol worship, sensorial experiences and the visual image are prominent in Hindu traditions of worship, they co-exist with ideas of virtual faith and non-phenomenological apprehensions of the divine; in this sense, the experience of the sacred is a virtual one (45). Against this backdrop, Saranam.com and Eprarthana.com strategically navigate a fine line by reproducing the idea of virtual devotion while simultaneously re-inscribing the authenticity of place and form-specific sensorial contexts for ritual worship.

Vmandir.com (virtual mandir/temple) exemplifies Hindu discourse sites which focus on the dissemination of Hindu philosophy, myth, and traditions of ritual practice. While the site employs sacred imagery (of deities, scriptures) and advances the idea of ritual forms of worship, it does not function as a homepage for any particular god in the Hindu tradition nor does it provide avenues to request pujas or other rituals. Predominantly text-based, vmandir.com is primarily interested in raising awareness about the spiritual and philosophical underpinnings of Hinduism and its ritual traditions. In doing so, vmandir.com foregrounds the Hindu temple as a virtual space of interaction between the divine and the human that exists outside and beyond the mediations of physical matter (temple structures, idol forms, priests, and material offerings).

II. Emergent practices and the politics of remediation

This section foregrounds three key practices – digital darshan, online rituals and virtual Hinduism – that are emergent in online Hindu temple cultures. It argues that temple sites exemplify the remediation of notions of digitality, network capital flows, hypertextuality and virtuality through the practices of digital darshan, online rituals and virtual Hinduism. These practices in turn constitute the elements of what I term 'desktop deities culture.'

Remediation as theorized by Bolter and Grusin refers to a refashioning that is a characterized by a 'dual logic' (55). Bolter and Grusin are most concerned with the ways in which new media involve the repurposing of 'older' media and also how the latter is refashioned to adapt to the new media environment. It is the dialogical relationship between digital media and analog media that contributes to the 'dual logic' whereby new media 'remediate and are remediated by their predecessors' (55). Bolter and Grusin use the term 'new' critically to locate a specific set of media practices, texts, technologies and institutions in a given historical moment, the present. Nevertheless, they are cognizant of the discursive politics of 'old' and 'new' categorizations that have shaped popular and institutional imaginings of media in general. Remediation is a useful concept in exploring Hindu temple sites because it offers the critical perspective to engage with the broader cultural, historical and institutional frameworks that underscore the textual, discursive and institutional strategies of Hindu temple websites.

Digital darshan refers to the online reconfiguration of the Hindu ritual tradition of darshan, commonly defined as the act of beholding the sacred image. The latter includes what Eck refers to as iconic Hindu images such as deities in anthropomorphic forms and aniconic ones where certain objects symbolize a particular divine presence (32). For example, an idol of the god Shiva is an iconic image while the smooth, cylindrical stone known as linga is his aniconic image. Eck includes photographs, calendar art and other mass-produced image reproductions of temples, idols, scriptures, pilgrimage sites and saints in her discussion of the Hindu sacred (32–58). Highlighting the dual functions of the image as focal point for mediation and embodiment of the divine, Eck elaborates:

> Since in the Hindu understanding, the deity is present in the image, the visual apprehension of the image is charged with religious meaning. Beholding the image is an act of worship, and through the eyes one gains the blessings of the divine. (Eck 3)

As Eck notes, multiplicity, simultaneity and symbolic representation characterize Hindu traditions of worship. The divine has various forms and names, multiple sacred images can be worshipped at the same time and temples and idols are ultimately symbolic representations of the divine presence (49). Rites of consecration play a key role in the transformation of the profane into the sacred, as they imbue physical time-space with the divine timelessness and presence (51–55). It is following such sacralization that the temple symbolizes the 'sacred whole of the cosmos' (73), and the inner sanctum its center; the act of entering a temple and making one's way to the inner most chamber to get a darshan of the presiding deity is thereby understood as a symbolic journey through the cosmos to its divine essence (63).

Digital darshan harnesses Web technologies and network space to represent the act of seeing the sacred image. HTA.org's strategy of visually depicting the temple's exterior on its main page while dispersing images (of idols, priests and ritual worship) from the temple's interior spaces across the site's hyperlinks is significant for its spatial-temporal framing of online darshan along the lines of a traditional visit to the temple where darshan of the temple is followed by darshan of its presiding deity as the visitor enters the temple and proceeds to its inner chambers. Navigating the hyperlinks, online devotees can receive darshan of multiple sacred images in a virtual sequence of their making. Digital darshan, in this regard, invokes and negotiates multiple spatial-temporal orders as the physical time-space frames shaping traditional understandings of temple-going intersect with the virtual time-space dimensions of network travel *and* the Hindu sacred. Even as it reminds the online devotee of the physical existence of the temple, HTA.org mobilizes digital darshan around the virtual apprehension of the sacred. Eprarthana.com's virtual puja for the god Balaji, where digitally created temple doors open to reveal the deity in his inner sanctum, offers a variation where physical symbols (temple exterior, doorways) construct the virtual navigation as a movement from profane (Web) to sacred (temple) space.[6] Vmandir.com, however, enables its visitors to have darshan of the site's presiding deities the moment the homepage is accessed. With its lack of attention to temples as physically bounded representations of sacred space, vmandir.com's version of digital darshan troubles the constructed divide between network and sacred space in which both HTA.org and Eprarthana.com participate. Given that for vmandir.com, the temple *is* a virtual space, darshan is not deployed to conjure up a physical memory of entering sacred space.

The nature of the image is also significant here. While digital imaging where the representation exists only in the form of bits is getting fairly common, there continues to be a great emphasis on 'traditional' forms such as photographs, paintings and Hindu calendar art that occupy a central place in popular Hindu culture. Digital darshan foregrounds the remediation of 'digital' as analog media forms such as the photograph, iconic calendar art and books are reconfigured as digital bits. Correspondingly, computer-generated images are fashioned along the lines of traditional representations of the 'sacred' in photographic or calendar art traditions; here iconic 'old media' imagery is purposefully used to sacralize the 'new' digital representation. In thinking about the politics of the remediated image, Bolter and Grusin's insights on the changing status of the image are worth considering:

> Ideally, there should be no difference between the experience of seeing a painting in person and on the computer screen, but this is never so. The computer always intervenes and makes its presence felt in some way.... (Bolter and Grusin 45–46)

At one level, the intervention is that the computer, like preceding mass-produced calendar art technologies, is extending the reach of the sacred image. While the scope and scale of that reach can be interrogated in different ways (for example, does the computer create a new divide?), it is important to point to the democraticizing potential of the virtual sacred image and consequently, digital darshan. As briefly stated earlier, while heterogeneity marks Hinduism, the orthodox Vedic ritual-intensive tradition has historically upheld Brahmin male spiritual privilege and mobilized ideologies of pollution to police Hindu women's ritual space and exclude 'lower-caste' members of society not merely from temple worship and darshan but, as Vijay Prashad notes, from the very category of 'Hindu' (553). The patriarchal nature of this tradition is also evidenced through the institutionalized practice of Brahmin males only as temple priests and in the notion that despite active roles in home-based rituals, women lack the 'scriptural sanction' to be seen as religious authorities (Wadley 121). Online darshan delinks the temple institution historically erected on caste and gender oppression from the practice to 'see and be seen by the deity' (Eck 3); new barriers (such as lack of network access) notwithstanding, it is significant that digital darshan opens up the space for historically marginalized Hindu subjects to renegotiate their relation to sacred space-time and divine presence.

Online rituals, the key second practice, are informed by the twin processes of (a) virtualization of rituals and (b) ritualization of the virtual. By *virtualization of rituals*, I refer to e-rituals like the virtual pujas on Eprarthana.com where ritualized modes of worship migrate online. *Ritualization of the virtual* refers to the manner in which the logic of the homepage is mobilized around Hindu organizations, beliefs and ritual elements. Online rituals are significant for their remediation of new media capital and network flows as Hindu capital and commodity flows.

While predominantly a commercial site, Eprarthana.com offers its 'virtual pujas' as freebies.[7] Two reminders posted for the users of the free puja service point to an interesting duality that eprarthana.com tries to negotiate – one tells the user to turn up the speakers for an audio chant during the e-ritual, the other clarifies that the virtual puja is unconnected to the puja orders processed by the site. The 'click and pray' audio-enhanced e-puja recreates ritual actions and sounds to engender a virtual sensorium of worship, yet its potential for creating personalized spaces of ritual worship is restrained by the site's overarching desire to capitalize on the institutionalized and priestly modes of worship. Further, the strategic advertising (for Hindu art and pilgrimage) alongside the free pujas highlights a common e-commerce site practice whereby freebies are used to construct a narrative of personalized interactivity even as their space is being simultaneously targeted to generate more revenue to the site (Miller 113–21).

While e-rituals illustrate the servicing of commerce through freebies, the ritualization of the virtual more forcefully exemplifies Hindu capital and commodity flows, or what Sangita Gopal has called, 'Hindu Buying, Hindu Being' (161–79). In her discussion of online Hindutva, Gopal contends that Saranam.com and Eprarthana.com, where 'Hindu practice … mutates into Hindu commodity' (174–75) participate in the global project of Hindutva by sharing the latter's logic that Hindu identity can be purchased. Following Gopal, I argue that both sites amplify the ritualization of the virtual where homepages and web economies are imagined around the servicing of temple institutions, Hindu devotees, and faith-based beliefs and rituals. The Web is the temple's destination and the homepage its updated identity. Localized temple spaces embodied in deities, priests and ritual forms of worship are now network-accessible while the temple organizations themselves are actively forging links with e-commerce enterprises. On their respective homepages, Saranam.com claims that 'thousands of devout Hindus trust and come back to Saranam for their needs', while Eprarthana.com succinctly maintains that it is 'the divine link.' The implication here is that both sites function as virtual priests, mediating globalized Hindus' relations with the divine. Displacing but not entirely replacing the centrality of the temple priest and puja through their key services, Saranam.com and Eprarthana.com discursively construct interaction with their sites as virtual acts of Hindu devotion. To pray at a given temple in India, one need only travel to the puja sites, click on the specific hyperlink, receive darshan, activate a shopping cart, order a customized puja and avail of the divine blessings (prasad) arriving by mail. In the process, both sites invent rituals of network interactivity as constitutive of the contemporary Hindu. While shopping carts with their multiple currency-pricings underscore the transnational base of Hindu capital, the recasting of ritual stages of worship as 'products' that can be Google-searched, purchased, tracked and shipped online highlight emergent contours of Hindu commodity flows. Forging links between traditional spaces of Hindu faith (temples) with contemporary symbols of capital and communication flows (the digital capitalist Web), puja sites engender the ritualization of the virtual and in turn, the remediation of new media capital and commodities as transnational Hindu capital and network flows.[8]

Ritualized virtual and capital flows summon ideas of place and traditional time-space relations to the fore, if only to negotiate and reconfigure them. Saranam.com for all its emphasis on online ritual activities continues to underscore traditional contexts of embodied and ritual time-space. For example, customers are reminded multiple times that the puja will be conducted at the time/date requested and that the site's representative, 'an authentic person ... who stays in close proximity to the temple will be present at the temple on behalf of the customer.'[9] Additionally, while an online puja order is theoretically an instant transaction, the shipped product/prasad permits the navigation of local courier and international mail time as the prasad travels from temple to Saranam's Chennai headquarters to customer (often located outside India).[10] The interactions of digital networks with traditional communication networks such as the telegraph, the telephone, and posted mail as evidenced in Saranam.com's multiple stage processing of the puja order serves to destabilize conventional understandings of the seamless flows of new media networks; networks do not overcome traditional time-space relations (in place) but flow through and around them. Speaking of place, the physical temple, a traditional embodiment of the sacred, is transformed to the extent that its interactions with ideas of virtual faith (understood both in the sense of in-absentia worship as well as the nature of human-divine interaction) are intensified and expanded. While in-absentia prayers are a part of the temple tradition, puja websites invoke them as central modes of contemporary worship.'Similarly, with temples being accessible 24/7 online, traditions of the sacred as inherently virtual are reinforced. As temples negotiate their identities and boundaries in the digital capitalist, transnational age, they open up possibilities for new modes and communities of faith. The idea that one does not physically have to visit a temple to patronize it is bolstered even as it reminds one that to be Hindu is to conduct rituals, and offer temple-centric worship.

The transformation of place informs the third key practice of virtual Hinduism on temple sites. I use the term virtual Hinduism to refer to the strategic articulation of Hindu-ness to aspects or elements of new media. In particular, virtual Hinduism, I argue, remediates ideas of virtuality and hypertexts within its logic even as it forges new alliances between Hindu temples and online cultures. In their discussion of new media, Lister et al. state that one of the key traditions of virtuality is informed by 'the metaphorical "places" and "spaces" created by or within communication networks' (35).[11] Vmandir.com with its emphasis on sacred word, text and image rather than temples *per se* offers a good example of the same. While the concept of the mandir (temple) frames the site, it functions to highlight Heinz Scheifinger's point that 'the belief in non-physical sacred spaces ... [is] entrenched in Hinduism' (235–36). Hence, upon clicking on a deity image to 'enter' the temple, one enters the realm of Hindu discourse constituted by Hindu art, text of sacred verses and hymns, description of ritual and their meaning. By shifting attention away from the physical representation of a temple and focusing on it as a virtual space of divine presence, vmandir.com deploys the homepage to service both new media and Hindu traditions of virtuality.

By flexibly articulating the temple-place to new media spaces shaped by migration, e-commerce and virtual worship, HTA.org, Saranam.com, Eprarthana.com and vmandir.com together demonstrate a virtual Hinduism that is becoming increasingly crucial to the globalizing mission of contemporary Hinduism. The migration of temple cultures onto an online environment highlights the remediation of virtuality as homepages become newer iterations of place. On HTA.org, one can only sign online to attend Sunday school or volunteer at the temple; one cannot be an online volunteer or attend a virtual classroom.[12] Likewise, even as Eprarthana.com pushes its virtual wares through features like 'temple of the day' or 'coming soon, xyz pujas,' the site is also a remarkable ode to an exhaustive list of temples in India whose histories are briefly delineated in a narrative that displays the temple's physical architecture as well as local myths surrounding the deity and temple location. Hindu temple sites, on the one hand, invite the online Hindu to consider the act of being virtually devout as a contemporary expression of an older tradition where place, image, ritual function as symbolic expressions of virtual faith. On the other hand, they re-inscribe the idea that a physical journey to the temple is a central mode of Hindu worship.

Nevertheless, the reconfiguration of the temple as a network-accessible Hindu space on Saranam.com and Eprarthana.com involves a strategic balancing of established spaces of temple worship (India's sacred, historic temples) with emergent ones (online and diasporic forms). India-based Saranam.com claims that a majority of its clients live overseas; in an interview, site co-founder Jose referred to his clientele as being 'too busy or too distant to go to a temple' (Pandey B09). Saranam.com's imagining of its target audience as diasporic Hindus becomes all the more significant when read in light of the rise of new media cultures on the one hand, and temple building in the diaspora on the other hand (Fairbanks). While sites like HTA.org highlight Hindu temples in US locales as well as its virtual forms, Saranam.com and its competitor Eprarthana.com tell us that new media play a critical function in re-routing expressions of Hindu ritualism to the 'hub' of sacred temples in India, thereby reinstating the Hindu Indian nation-space as the 'original' and 'authentic' space of a global diaspora.

Virtual Hinduism also refashions the hypertext in the process of reinventing the temple as a series of navigable links. Shaped by conventions of intertextuality and data linking, the hypertext, 'a work which is made up from discrete units of material in which each one carries a number of pathways to other units' (Lister et al. 23–24) complicates ideas of space and time since in terms of access, each link is theoretically 'equidistant from the reader' (24). With features like mobile accessible order forms, puja sites invested in linking Indian temples with overseas Hindus signal that distance is easily navigable, making India-based temples as accessible, if not more so, as overseas-based ones. Considering that temples in the diaspora (including the US-based HTA) labor to construct their authenticity by suggesting that they replicate the 'original' located in India, it is possible to read the puja sites' marketing of access as an invitation to pursue the original rather than its replica. Elaborating on the politics of the hypertextual Web, Rob Shields argues that

> Webpages are not browsed as static texts, but in motion – even in the simplest manner, as one scrolls down the length of a webpage. This sense of mobility lies in the nature of the bricolage of elements and of hypertexts links as 'indexes' – semiotic pointers to a fuller presentation (such as another webpage) that they announce, indicate or prefigure. (146)

Hindu temple sites through their practice of virtual Hinduism certainly invoke the idea of linkages, motion and intertextuality embedded within this understanding of hypertext. Given the fact that temple cultures are organized around auspicious times, dates, months and events, the temple sites' coverage of ritual activity is constantly in motion. For instance, in early 2009, Saranam.com advertised a ritual for economic prosperity by making a reference to the global recession. More importantly, a link for Sunday school activities on HTA.org points to the evolving politics of temples in the US; as Arvind Rajagopal (467–96) and Vinay Lal (98–138) have observed, US temples are increasingly operating as 'cultural' institutions and playing an active role in the construction of a Hindu Indian American identity.

At the same time, the hypertextual Web perceived in terms of equal nodes, mobility, and decentered non-place is being reconfigured by virtual Hindu practices that to an extent highlight traditional time-space relations and materiality of places and rituals. On HTA.org online requests for donations, the temple president's e-address, the virtual archive of the temple's history and an online announcement page for the temple's key everyday activities solidify the online existence of the temple. Nevertheless, the site maintains an emphasis on the Riverdale location by mobilizing hypertextual links to enact, describe and reference the materiality and time-space relations of the physical setting, best exemplified through its 'History' section.[13] Here documents organized around photographs, quotations, original documents and research literature reconstruct the temple's beginning as an 'idea' and conclude with the temple consecration. The linear narrative revolves around key moments depicted by separate and chronologically listed links; the 'history' that happened between the beginning and the end is represented by links about principles of Indian temple construction, temple plans and sketches, arrival of the sculptors from India, Indianization of the temple (an architectural concept driven by faithfulness to Indian temple styles), arrival of deities and ritual consecration of deities. It is important to note that while the dominant narrative here privileges a sequential, chronological history, given the hypertextual character of the page, one could very well view the history in a non-linear, incomplete, and partial way. In this sense, the hypertext functions as both an agent of structured narrative and also its revelation (as in pointing to the constructed nature of the narrative), through a possible eliding of the preferred sequence by the Web user.

Conclusion

This study has examined Hindu temples on the Web by focusing on three key types, the temple homepage, the commercial puja site and the Hindu discourse site. It has argued that Hindu temple sites demonstrate the emergence of what I call 'desktop deity culture' constituted through the practices of digital darshan, online rituals and virtual Hinduism. These online practices exemplify the 'remediation' (Bolter and Grusin) of new media conceptualizations of digitality, network capital flows, hypertextuality and virtuality as they are articulated to ideas of the Hindu image, embodied ritual practice and the temporal and spatial logic of the temple as sacred place. Hindu temple sites repurpose 'older' media forms such as Hindu calendar art through their textual and discursive practices of representing online temples. Likewise, hypertextual connectivity, virtual forms of dis/embodiment and im/materiality and mobile flows of capital and culture are deployed to pay service to place-centric, embodied and material practices shaping Hindu temple cultures. In this remediation of Hindu representational forms and material practices with new media ideologies and practices, both Hindu temples and new media as cultural forms are reinvented as 'desktop deity cultures.' A significant aspect of the virtualization of temple cultures is the potential democratization engendered as historically marginalized women and 'lower-caste' Hindu subjects re-imagine their relation to a ritual space that has traditionally been an upper-caste male bastion. Another pertinent aspect, only briefly addressed here but deserving further analysis, is the complicity of virtual temple sites in the shaping of a global brand of Hinduism characterized by homogeneity, commodification and transnational mobility. Further, as Hindus in the US are key target audiences/users for temple sites, it becomes important to examine how virtual temple cultures complicate the relations between Indian American imaginings of 'community' and Hindu-centric notions of identity. Drawing, for example, on critical scholarship that has pointed to the hegemonic position of the Hindu immigrant within narratives of Indian American identity (Prashad *Karma*; Lal; Rajagopal; Maira; Desai), and the temple Sunday School's politicization through an active alliance with proponents of the right wing Hindutva ideology (Rayaprol; Rangaswamy), one can interrogate how virtual temples reinforce established or engender new elements of US temple cultures at large. While this article has focused on the new media practices of Hindu temple sites, the latter's cultural politics for Indian American imaginations of Hindu identity and community; while outside the scope of this paper, is a significant issue that warrants thorough analysis.

Notes

1. The tagline of www.eprarthana.com
2. A reference to this experiment dated 18 November 2002 can be found in the online news archives of Department of Philosophy and Religious Studies at Iowa University: http://www.las.iastate.edu/newnews/sanford1118.shtml. The link taking one to the direct research site has been made inaccessible currently.
3. http://www.hindutempleofatlanta.org/AboutHistory.aspx
4. http://www.saranam.com/astrology/
5. http://www.saranam.com/pujas/puja_product.asp?TempleID=750 shows the shopping cart and order page for Mumbai's Siddhivinayak Temple, one of India's most famous Ganesh temples.
6. http://www.eprarthana.com/virtual/vbalaji.asp
7. http://www.eprarthana.com/virtual/vpooja.asp
8. Drawing on Aihwa Ong's discussion of transnationality (4), I use transnationality to denote both the condition of moving beyond the nation as well as connecting across nation-spaces.
9. http://www.saranam.com/help/help3.htm
10. http://www.saranam.com/Help/help18.htm
11. The notion of 'immersive' conceived in Lister et al.'s categorization privileges a technologically determined conceptualization of immersiveness. While not extremely relevant to the discussion at hand, suffice to say here that such a conceptualization is debatable in light of nuanced understandings of new media experiences of mobility and feeling 'at place.'
12. http://www.hindutempleofatlanta.org/Balavihar.aspx
13. http://www.hindutempleofatlanta.org/AboutHistory.aspx

Notes on contributor

Madhavi Mallapragada is assistant professor in the Department of Radio-Television-Film at the University of Texas at Austin. She is currently working on a book that explores Indian American identities in the age of online media.

References

Bolter, Jay David, and Richard Grusin. *Remediation: Understanding New Media*. Cambridge, MA: MIT Press, 1999. Print.

Brasher, Brenda E. *Give me that Online Religion*. New Brunswick: Rutgers, 2004. Print.

Campbell, Heidi. *Exploring Religious Community Online: We are One in the Network*. New York: Peter Lang, 2005. Print.

Dawson, Lorne, and Douglas Cowan. *Religion Online: Finding Faith on the Internet*. London: Routledge, 2004. Print.

Desai, Jigna. *Beyond Bollywood: The Cultural Politics of South Asian Diasporic Film*. New York: Routledge, 2004. Print.

Eck, Diana L. *Darsan: Seeing the Divine Image in India*. 3rd ed. New York: Columbia UP, 1998. Print.

Fairbanks, Amanda M. "For Hindus, New Temples are a Sign of Having Arrived." *The New York Times Online* 4 Jun. 2008. Web. 10 May 2009. <http://cityroom.blogs.nytimes.com/2008/06/04/for-hindus-new-temples-are-a-sign-of-having-arrived/>.

Gopal, Sangita. "Hindu Being, Hindu Buying: Hindutva Online and the Commodity Logic of Late Nationalism." *South Asian Review* 24.1 (2003): 161–79. Print.

Helland, Christopher. "Surfing for Salvation." *Religion* 32.3 (2002): 293–302. Web. 24 Feb. 2009.

Helland, Christopher. "Religion Online/Online Religion and Virtual Communitas." *Religion on the Internet: Research Prospects and Promises*. Ed. Jeffrey K. Hadden and Douglas E. Cowan. London: JAI Press/Elsevier Science, 2004. 205–24. Print.

Helland, Christopher. "Online Religion as Lived Religion: Methodological Issues in the Study of Religious Participation on the Internet." *Heidelberg Journal of Religions on the Internet* 1.1 (2005): n. pag. Web. 24 Feb. 2009.

Jacobs, Stephen. "Virtually Sacred: The Performance of Asynchronous Cyber-Rituals in Online Spaces." *Journal of Computer-Mediated Communication* 12 (2007): 1103–21. Web. 24 Feb. 2009.

Lal, Vinay. "North American Hindus, the Sense of History, and the Politics of Internet Diasporism." *AsianAmerica.Net: Ethnicity, Nationalism, and Cyberspace*. Ed. Rachel C. Lee and Sau-Ling Cynthia Wong. New York: Routledge, 2003. 98–138. Print.

Lister, Martin et al. *New Media: A Critical Introduction*. London: Routledge, 2003. Print.

Maira, Sunaina Marr. *Desis in the House: Indian American Youth Culture in New York City*. Philadelphia: Temple UP, 2002. Print.

Miller, Vincent. "Search Engines, Portals and Global Capitalism." *Web.studies: Rewiring Media Studies for the Digital Age*. Ed. David Gauntlett. London: Arnold, 2000. 113–21. Print.

O'Leary, Stephen D. "Cyberspace as Sacred Space: Communicating Religion on Computer Networks." *Journal of the American Academy of Religion* 64.4 (1996): 781–808. Web. 24 Feb. 2009.

Ong, Aihwa. *Flexible Citizenship: The Cultural Logics of Transnationality*. Durham: Duke UP, 1999. Print.

Pandey, Onkar. "Hindus go online for Festival blessings; Prayers, Incense available on Web." *The Washington Post* 7 Oct. 2006: B 09. Web. 15 Jan. 2009. <http://www.lexisnexis.com.ezproxy.lib.utexas.edu/hottopics/inacademic/>.

Prashad, Vijay. "The Untouchable Question." *Economic and Political Weekly* 31.9 (1996): 551–9. Web. 2 Jan. 2010. <http://www.jstor.org/stable/4403863>.

Prashad, Vijay. *The Karma of Brown Folk*. Minnesota: U of Minnesota P, 2000. Print.

Rajagopal, Arvind. "Hindu Nationalism in the US: Changing Configurations of Political Practice." *Ethnic and Racial Studies* 23.3 (2000): 467–96. Web. 15 Jan. 2009. <http://dx.doi.org/10.1080/014198700328953>.

Ramo, Joshua Cooper, and Greg Burke. "Finding God on the Web." *Time Online* 16 Dec. 1996. Web. 10 May 2009.

Rangaswamy, Padma. *Namastè America: Indian Immigrants in an American Metropolis*. University Park, PA: Penn State UP, 2000. Print.

Rayaprol, Aparna. *Negotiating Identities: Women in the Indian Diaspora*. New Delhi: Oxford UP, 1997. Print.

Scheifinger, Heinz. "Hinduism and Cyberspace." *Religion* 38 (2008): 233–49. Web. 24 Jan. 2009. <http://dx.doi.org/10.1016/j.religion.2008.01.008>.

Shields, Rob. "Hypertext Links: The Ethic of the Index and its Space-Time Effects." *The World Wide Web and Contemporary Cultural Theory*. Ed. Andrew Herman and Thomas Swiss. New York: Routledge, 2000. 145–60. Print.

Sink, Mindy. "Religion Journal; Now Available: Spiritual Connection on the Internet." *The New York Times* 28 Dec. 2002. B1: 6. Web. 15 Jan. 2009. <http://ezproxy.lib.utexas.edu/login?url=http://search.ebscohost.com/login.aspx?direct=true&db=a9h&AN=29114504&site=ehost-live>.

Taparia, Nidhi. "Hurry Om! God Lives in Cyberspace and He downloads real fast!" *India Abroad* 3 Aug. 2001. 31.44: M 15. Web. 15 Jan. 2009. <http://proquest.umi.com.ezproxy.lib.utexas.edu/pqdweb?did=490991721&sid=3&Fmt=3-&clientid=48776&RQT=309&VName=PQD>.

Wadley, Susan S. "Women and the Hindu Tradition." *Signs* 3.1 (1977): 113–25. Web. 15 Dec. 2009. <http://www.jstor.org/stable/3173084>.

Some annotations on the film festival as an emerging medium in India

Pooja Rangan

Department of Modern Culture and Media, Brown University, Providence, USA

> Organized around an interview with the curator of the 2009 Ahmedabad International Film Festival in India, this article inventories a number of issues germane to future discussions of the film festival as an emerging exhibition venue in India. I examine some of the existing theoretical and critical models for analyzing film festivals, and argue that the film festival should be considered as a 'medium' that behaves as a productive constraint on both film production and spectatorship. Finally, I consider the unique relation between the spectatorial behaviors encouraged within festival settings and the narrative strategies of Indian popular films, so as to interrogate their impact on the cultivation of a critically-oriented Indian film audience. I conclude by evaluating the promises and challenges of the infrastructural limitations faced by Indian film festivals for the emergence of alternative cinema publics.

A prefatory note

Investigating the film festival in India presents a curious problem. One is confronted with an overabundance of archival material: catalogs, press clippings, posters, program notes, news stories, and interviews with jury members, filmmakers, and movie stars. Film festivals endlessly monumentalize themselves in architectural reams of media records, so much so that film scholar Daniel Dayan once proclaimed them to be impossible objects of study, since they are not only performative phenomena – scripts subject to reinterpretation by each participant – but also archival behemoths (see Dayan 43–52). The flipside of this is that there is very little theoretical or critical material written on film festivals in general (although this has been changing in the past decade), and as yet no definitive piece of writing on film festivals in India, even though film festivals themselves are on the rise. The last 20 years have witnessed the emergence of a number of new forums for exhibiting cinema in India, forums that are ushering in new forms of filmmaking, generic experimentation, and spectatorship. One major and very visible change across urban landscapes throughout the country is the sweeping entrance of multi-screen entertainment complexes, accompanied by the slow obsolescence of neighborhood single-screen theaters. The advent of multiplex culture in the mid-1990s coincides with the popularity of what Ashish Rajadhyaksha and Madhava Prasad have dubbed 'Bollywood,' an ambitious genre of films that address a transnational and upwardly mobile audience – together, these developments are argued to reflect new intensities in the global aspirations and imaginations of middle-class urban and small-town Indian audiences (see Rajadhyaksha 25–39; Prasad). However, alongside these shifts in mainstream film culture, there have also been a number of less conspicuous but nonetheless significant transformations in what we might call, for the lack of a better word, the alternative cinematic public sphere in India.

Key among these, and the focus of this paper, is an unprecedented proliferation and institutionalization of regional, genre-specific, and special-interest film festivals and film series all over the country in the last 15 years.

Since approximately 1995, a number of state-sponsored, independent, and corporate-funded film festivals have taken root in urban centers, displacing the monopoly of the Indian government's now 40 year-old IFFI (International Film Festival of India) over the province of the film festival. The Kolkata Film Festival was founded in 1995, and others soon followed suit – the Kerala International Film Festival (1996), Madurai Film Festival (1998), MIFF (Mumbai International Film Festival, 1998), Osian's Cinefan in Delhi (1999), Pune International Film Festival (2003), Chennai International Film Festival (2003), and Ahmedabad International Film Festival (2009). In addition to cultivating and showcasing independent films, foreign films, 'offbeat films,' regional cinema, and premiering select mainstream movies (often those on the fringes of the mainstream), several of these bigger-budget forums have dedicated themselves to providing exhibition opportunities for specific genres that do not receive wide theatrical release – documentary in the case of Madurai and MIFF; Asian and Arab cinema in the case of Osian's. A number of affinity-based smaller and co-op-style spaces have also cropped up in recent years, organized around political and genre interests. Examples include the climate-oriented Monsoon Film Festival (2005) and Vatavaran Environment and Wildlife Film Festival (2006), Experimenta International Festival for Experimental Cinema (2003), the Vikalp Film Series (2004; founded by documentary filmmakers to protest censorship policies at MIFF), Mocha (2003) and Shamiana (2009) Short Film Clubs, and Persistence Resistance (2008; a festival dedicated to social justice and activist films, organized by Magic Lantern Foundation, the only distributor of independent cinema in India). This list represents just some of the established annual film festivals and regular series. I have not even begun to inventory the more irregular, occasional, or one-time events, which would comprise a far longer catalog. Suffice to say that the film festival is now more than simply a new medium for the exhibition and advocacy of non-mainstream Indian films and international cinema – it has become a staple of urban experience in India, one whose spatial organization, temporal intensities, and rhetorics of generic celebration are instrumental in producing new architectures of film production and spectatorship in India.

While it may be too early to make any definitive statements about these developments, which are still relatively new, the changes they are engendering demand to be theorized. The film festival is still relatively unexplored in academic scholarship about cinema, despite an abundance of riches in terms of raw material – there is a rich and long tradition of film festivals in Europe and the USA, and a high degree of sophistication in popular discourses of the film festival, which is now a highly diversified form in the West. What scholarship does exist is very recent and often limited in scope. As I will detail in the sections that follow, research on the film festival tends to take film critical forms or follow in the revisionist-historicist tradition of Dutch film historian Thomas Elsaesser, and both kinds of discourses ultimately shy away from the task of engaging the film festival dialectically, as a medium that actively shapes and restructures not only the medium of film, but also what we understand as 'cinema,' in all of its dimensions, including spectatorship, questions of stardom, and cinema's own enduring cultural logic. Following are a brief set of annotations that attempt to address some of these problematics. My comments do not purport to fill the gap in the scholarship on film festivals in India or critique the state of scholarship on film festivals in any conclusive or authoritative sense – the absence of a conclusion to this article is deliberate – although I do hope to contribute to a conversation that is only just beginning. Most of all, I want to pose a set of provocations, which were in turn provoked by an interview that I conducted with filmmaker and curator Ajitpal Singh, the Director of Programming for the 2009 Ahmedabad International Film Festival (AIFF). AIFF held its first session this summer and, in Singh's own account, 'failed' as a festival. Singh's reflections on the difficulties of mounting, and furthermore, sustaining this fairly ambitious film festival led me to formulate a number of problematics that target some of the key issues that cluster around the film festival in India as both a practical endeavor and an object of study. These are certainly not the only methodologies through which to approach the topic, but they represent privileged sites of inquiry for me in that they are located at the nexus of theoretical concerns and the issues of feasibility addressed by Singh, which are in the last instance, issues of a cultural base. Importantly, I want to argue this is a critical and ripe time for making such a double-pronged intervention: AIFF may have 'failed' at an empirical level – mostly the result of a gap between the global scale of the festival organizers' ambitions and the nascent level of the actual infrastructure available to realize them – but this 'failure' bears a wealth of potential in that it opens up a rich set of issues for critical inquiry and reflection.

The interview with Singh is located at the end of the paper, and it can be read first or last, as the reader pleases – I refer to it often in my various annotations.

The festival that failed

After nearly two years of preparation, the Ahmedabad International Film Festival took place from 25 to 28 June 2009. AIFF featured films in three competitive sections judged by a jury composed of Indian filmmakers, television personalities, and stage actors: Independent Feature Films, Fictional/Live Action Short Films, and Documentary Films. In addition, the festival also solicited specially curated sets of films from the Berlin Film Festival and Tampere Film Festival, and included programs dedicated to the regional cinema of Gujarat, films dealing with AIDS, and children's films. Originally slated to be sponsored and hosted at Wide Angle, a local movie multiplex, the festival organizers had to seek a new venue a mere month before the event began – like many others, AIFF was caught in the cross-fire between multiplex owners and film producers that resulted in the famous multiplex strike in India from April to June 2009. Unlike their old exhibition partner, AIFF's new sponsor FullMarxx would not subsidize the cost of ticketing, so large numbers of spectators were turned away by the high price of tickets even though most screenings ran at far less than full capacity. Consequently the festival was poorly attended. The festival also featured a film market named the 'Independent Film Bazaar' – a separate space dedicated to fostering transactions between filmmakers and potential distributors, studio representatives, exhibitors, and TV executives. A guest speaker event was scheduled for each day of the festival, but other than that the Film Bazaar was a fairly unstructured space; although it was an active social networking site for the filmmakers and guest speakers in attendance, very few distribution deals were actually struck.

The black box and the white cube, or, the question of the medium

The account below by Ajitpal Singh is typical of discussions of film festivals, which invariably amount to a series of opinions culled together from personal recollection, autobiographical interlude, and anecdote. In addressing the synecdochic tendencies and highly confessional impulses that seem to emerge in response to the task of taking stock of the film festival, Richard Porton has remarked that accounts of film festivals are 'intermittently gratifying, frequently maddening,' and nearly always resemble a genre of travel writing (see Porton 1). There is a word for this kind of account. It is a cinephilic account – a chronicle punctuated by revelatory moments, but one that ultimately shies away from the task of articulating the particular to the whole. Specificity and the totality are called upon in alternation, but rarely dialectically. The proliferation of film festivals and screening spaces in cities across the world (and as Singh demonstrates, India is no exception) seems to trigger a mimetic impulse toward the proliferation of example and opinion in critique. The film festival seems to have become the purview of film criticism rather than film theory, with the result that there is a widespread avoidance of critical frameworks that attend to text *and* context – frameworks which would seek to attend to questions of the specificity of the film festival as a medium for producing an encounter between film texts and actors with various stakes in the films.

Film scholar Marijke de Valck – whose recent book *Film Festivals: From European Geopolitics to Global Cinephilia* has been publicized as the first 'definitive' book-length study of film festivals – advocates actor-network theory (ANT), developed by science studies scholar and anthropologist Bruno Latour, as a model that provides a global perspective on the stakes of film festivals in an era where global flows have replaced cultural-territorial segments. This, she argues, is a necessary 'update' to the earlier era of more traditionally anthropological film-critical work on film festivals by Danial Dayan and Kenneth Turan (see Dayan 43–52; Turan). De Valck argues that ANT attends to the 'hybrid connections' between the various 'antagonistic and constitutive' forces acting in film festivals (De Valck 29). Moreover, by rejecting the conceptual distinction between human and non-human actors, ANT moves away from the problematic dichotomizing tendencies of 1970s apparatus theory's ideological schemas, and is able to account for the agendas of various entities that converge in the film festival, such as cinephiles, casual audiences, film industry professionals, government officials with business agendas and/or political purposes, programmers, and the press (30–31). The downside of adopting this 'non-hierarchical' model for analyzing film festivals, as De Valck admits, is that ANT is unable to address the ideological *stakes* of film festivals, or as she puts it, the 'neo-colonial tendencies that persist in the new configurations' (214).

De Valck leads us to a compelling problem: how do we theorize the ideological operations of the film festival given that the 'black box' of the theater experience has been exploded – not only by the arrival of video and television, but also by the film festival's openness to a multiplicity of performances and agendas? In other words, how can we begin to talk about how the film festival functions not just as a medium in the sense of a channel, vehicle, or environment for the presentation of film, but as a medium in every sense of Foucault's notion of a *dispositif* or apparatus? The theoretically oriented writings of art historians such as Rosalind Krauss, James Putnam, and Brian O'Doherty on the museum and the art gallery as mediums provide variations on a model that may be productive for thinking about the film festival (Krauss 3–17; Putnam; O'Doherty). This model has particular theoretical currency in that it points out that the content of art programming has become inextricable from its exhibition content. If we follow Krauss's insights, we can see how in postmodernity, the spheres of context and content can no longer be considered separate or immiscible.

De Valck's reluctance to isolate the individual film text as a unit through which cultural meaning is produced argues the relevance of this problematic for contemporary discussions of the film festival. Questioning along these lines, we might ask: In what ways does the film festival structure the experience of film viewing, or rather, film consumption? What kinds of new relations to space and time are produced by the specific scale, seriality, and intensities of festival programming, as opposed to the more occasional and isolated programming of special interest film groups and series? Is there a value in abstracting a general 'script' that film festivals follow, so that we might then investigate how this is re-enacted and transformed within various national and local configurations? Moreover, perhaps most significantly, how can we adapt these questions – without dismissing them altogether – for talking about the distinctly postmodern experience of the contemporary international film festival?

'Darshan': The auratic look in the Indian film festival

A well-known Indian documentary filmmaker I know recently posted a humorous post on her blog regarding a Freudian slip in a misspelled signpost at the Delhi office of the Indian Directorate of Film Festivals (co-sponsor of the International Film Festival of India). Caricaturing the sign, which reads, 'Way to Office of the Film Print Unit, Directorte of Film Festivals,' she suggests that perhaps this is 'the government's inimitable way of reminding filmmakers that you can't have your torte and eat it too ... it's art or commerce baby; success or goodness.' She continues, 'Unless of course you go to another kind of festival altogether, and get some special boons,' and includes a picture of a billboard publicizing a religious gathering.[1]

This jestful comment revisits a conversation Walter Benjamin began nearly a century ago, in 1935, when he argued the disintegrating impact of the advent of film, as a technology of mechanical reproduction, on the status of art as a ritual object (Benjamin 'Work of Art'). It did not take long for film to take the place of painting as the source of an auratic encounter – in 1955, Andre Bazin would describe the experience of attending film festivals in the journal *Cahiers du cinèma* as a spiritual experience resembling a 'monastic retreat' (Bazin 13–19, reprinted in Porton 1–10).

For film scholar Ravi Vasudevan, this quasi-spiritual capacity of cinema to weave a collective spell over its audience has a special resonance when it comes to Indian cinema. Vasudevan has argued that an aesthetics of frontality and iconicity (also found in Indian calendar art and religious tableaux) is more operative in Indian films than a fetishistic narrative coding of address (Vasudevan 310–12). Accordingly, in Indian cinema, the gendered structure of looking, *darshan dena* and *darshan lena* – the power to give the look, and the privilege of receiving it – is inverted in relation to Hollywood films, where the female body is the privileged object of desire (313). Prototyped in early mythological films, the *darshanic* is mapped at the level of visual codes onto the power relation between the male deity and the female devotee. These narrative codes have persisted in reproducing gendered authority structures (such as son–mother, husband–wife, brother–sister, father–daughter, and so on) within subsequent genres of film narrative, including the melodrama. Significantly, Vasudevan argues, these gendered familial structures also subtend other kinds of imagined communal relations – particularly the spectator's identification with a national collectivity, or the motherland. The spectator's relation with the *film* as a *darshanic* or sacred object is another cornerstone of this theory (318–19).

Singh's comments in his interview reinforce the view of the blog post I just quoted: when it comes to the film festival, 'it's either art or commerce.' Inevitably, commerce takes first place, so that something essential about the religious nature of the encounter with film seems to have waned in the era of the film festival and its attendant age of digital reproduction. In fact, the attraction at many contemporary Indian film festivals is less the (often unknown, obscure, and unrecognizable) films and more the possibility of being in the god-like presence of that world-famous celebrity, the Bollywood film, quintessential vehicle of Benjamin's notion of the 'false aura.' Without becoming nostalgic about some lost original moment when film was 'purely art,' how can we begin to address this shift that the film festival produces in the status of film? What kinds of new spectatorial relations do emerging genres of independent Indian cinema (documentary, short films, and fiction features) engender? How does the programming of such films alongside Bollywood films, retrospectives of older genres of Indian cinema, and contemporary world cinema shape the kinds of textual encounters that take place at the site of film? How best can we theorize the imperative for a Bollywood celebrity presence at Indian film festivals that aspire to an 'international' scale and profile? How is the space of the film festival articulated in relation to the space of the nation and the 'world'? If the spectator of the kinds of films Vasudevan discusses is hailed to take up a position within a symbolic nation-space that is predominantly Hindu, then what kinds of new symbolic transactions do film festivals enable in relation to the day-to-day functions of the multiplex?

The cultural logic of the late-capitalist film festival

When asked to comment on the infrastructural obstacles facing film festivals in India, Singh responds without hesitation, 'there is no market for independent cinema in India.' The choice of the term 'market' rather than 'audience' is striking – as is the tendency to think of films not as texts but rather as assets, and of culture as a brand rather than a shared experience. Krauss argues that this kind of shift in the status of art as a cultural commodity is typical of the current late-capitalist moment, which is characterized by the penetration of industrial modes of production and consumption into spheres previously considered to be discrete, private, or outside the realm of capital including leisure, sport, and art. We can certainly observe the kinds of trends she observes regarding the 'late capitalist museum' operating within the film festival in India – the shift from public patrimony to corporate entity; the functioning of cultural products as assets rather than as ambassadors; the cultivation of a relationship with the mainstream, however reluctant; the increasingly centralized role of the curator as entrepreneur. This kind of logic is typical of late-capitalist cultural reprogramming, Krauss argues, where the imagined alternative spaces are 'shaped somehow by the structural features of the same nightmare' (Krauss 435).

What is striking about Singh's example of AIFF is not so much that the dominant notion of the film festival in India today is one that is more often than not identified as a space of commerce – this uneasy mix of aesthetic/political and commercial interests characterizes nearly all major international film festivals, including Berlin, Cannes, Venice, and so on. Rather, what is remarkable is that India seems to have bypassed an entire era in the history of the film festival, when the film festival was predominantly an avant-garde space for political struggle through art. Indeed as De Valck notes, the 'energizing spirit' of the 1920s and early 1930s European filmic avant-garde was responsible for galvanizing the earliest film festivals in Europe, whose models were later exported to the USA and beyond. For several decades, film festivals functioned as an agora, a radical alternative to Hollywood, offering

> ... non-commercial exhibition opportunities for all kinds of 'artistic' films from roughly 1919 onwards. The screenings were organized in order to nurture an intellectual vanguard and [to] more or less directly interfere in the film industry business by promoting alternative products and places of exhibition. (De Valck 25)

My point is not that such alternative or politically-minded festival spaces do not exist today in India – screening series such as Vikalp and Experimenta in Mumbai stand as testament to their existence, although they are relatively marginalized in comparison with the larger film festival events. Nor is it my intention to occupy the moral high ground and criticize the larger film festivals that envision and self-fashion themselves as markets for independent filmmakers to sell their product. The importance of a healthy fiscal infrastructure for supporting alternative forms and genres of film production is beyond question, but at the moment such an infrastructure barely exists in India. With the exception of the small revenue made possible to some by Magic Lantern Foundation (at the moment the sole pioneer in independent film distribution in India), most independent filmmakers rely on foreign film festival bookings for exposure and generating cultural capital, and international screenings and sales for generating income. The question is whether the failure of film festivals as markets is a sign that steps need to be taken first toward cultivating an *audience* for alternative modes of film practice – or in other words, a cultural base of conversation, debate, participation, and critique.

New openings

Cyrus Dastoor, co-founder of Shamiana Short Film Club, which is currently virally inaugurating new club 'chapters' in various cities and townships across Maharashtra and Gujarat, was among the four guest speakers (a list that included me) invited to speak at AIFF's market space, the *Independent Film Bazaar*. During his talk – which, like the rest of the bazaar, was attended mostly by young Indian makers of short films and some independent feature filmmakers – Dastoor suggested that the filmmakers use their short films as 'calling cards to get funding for larger films.' Not only did this simply not happen during AIFF – no short films received any kind of exhibition or distribution offers (not even on television, which is known to be notoriously exploitative of short-film makers) – but Dastoor's comment was met with a substantial amount of disagreement from some of the attending filmmakers, who argued that more venues for the short film as a new form of art are needed, in addition to funding and support for more traditional feature films. With no distributors in sight to speak to, the filmmakers continued this discussion of the short film as an avenue of communication rather than a form of currency during my talk, which followed immediately after Dastoor's. This then led to a very lively and engaged exchange on the film festival as a medium, during which several new and experimental models for improving the forum of the festival were proposed. Following this discussion, many of the filmmakers have remained in touch through an e-mail listserv, and now have a group on Facebook.

So perhaps another question we need to ask is: What if the failure of the market within the Indian film festival opens up space for new kinds of conversations about cinema and its futures? What are the possibilities, and the limits (channeling Singh's pessimistic comment below that discussions at film festivals are tantamount to manifestos for stopping global warming – all talk and no plausible action) of the kinds of supports for social networking that extend the interactions that may begin within the fora of film festivals? If the film festival in Indian can function as a new public sphere, then how can we take seriously the new textual forms and encounters (rather than assets) that it structures, limits, and enables – in other words, how can we account for its productive failures?

Interview with Ajitpal Singh – Director of Programming, Ahmedabad International Film Festival 2009

Pooja Rangan: How did you become involved in the 2009 Ahmedabad International Film Festival? Was it the first time you curated a festival of this scale?

Ajitpal Singh: Yes, it was a first for me. My involvement in AIFF was through Milap [Milapsingh Jadeja – a partner in the sponsor company]. Milap knew about my knowledge of world cinema and he knows that I am a regular at film festivals abroad. At the time, there was nobody who knew anything about film festivals. So he asked me to come on board.

We actually first tried to do a film festival in Ahmedabad in 2005. I went to Wide Angle [an entertainment complex and multiplex based in Ahmedabad] in 2005, and told them we wanted to mount a festival. I said, 'We'll invite films from all around the world... French films, Lebanese films, German films. Nobody has seen these kinds of films around here and I think there will be an audience for such films.' But Wide Angle wouldn't believe that somebody would actually come and watch a film from Iran, and Iraq. They asked, 'Why would people want to come and watch this kind of film?' So that was just the wrong time to approach them. And then things changed so much in four years

PR: What changed and how?

AS: Things changed mainly because of news channels – they started running news stories about Osian's Cinefan Film Festival, the Goa Film Festival, Berlin Film Festival. There are so many news channels in India now. They'll report anything exciting.

PR: So you think things changed because of the news media?

AS: Yes – there was so much coverage of film festivals in the media that people were suddenly aware on a different level about the phenomenon of film festivals.

PR: So what you're saying is that in 2005, although the artistic vision was there, the corporate institutions you approached to finance the film festival were not ready to invest in such a venture?

AS: I think even the audience may not have been ready at that time. Nobody really knew about film festivals in Ahmedabad. Nobody had any idea that there were other kinds of cinema apart from Bollywood and Hollywood... There are now two dedicated TV channels for foreign cinema in India [that came up in the intervening years]: NDTV Lumiere and UTV World Movies. So all this started and suddenly people were made aware that there are other kinds of cinema. Because of that, those people who could finance film festivals were suddenly ready to support something like that. When we pitched it again to Wide Angle a few years later, they accepted it. And that's how it happened.

PR: You said you thought the audience wasn't there in 2005. But haven't Osian's Cinefan and MIFF been taking place for over a decade now? Didn't the scene change with the emergence of Vikalp Documentary series and Cyrus Dastoor's Shamiana film club, which began as short film screenings at Café Mocha outlets around Mumbai? What's the difference between those venues and what you were trying to do?

AS: Cities such as Bombay, Delhi, Calcutta have had film festival cultures and film societies for over 50 years, since Independence times. Because they are metros, bigger cities, and people there are aware of different kinds of cinema. Bombay happened to be the city of film. And Delhi has pretty much displaced Calcutta as the cultural capital of India. But in Ahmedabad, festival-style events are only ever held in NID [the National Institute of Design], and sometime the Alliance Francaise – but were really only attended by students from NID and IIM [Indian Institute of Management].

PR: So film festival culture is mostly a student culture in such smaller cities?

AS: Yes. And never a mainstream culture. So that was the reason Ahmedabad was not ready in 2005. And this is true of almost all second-tier Indian cities. Now smaller cities like Indore, Bhopal, and even Surat are doing film festivals.

PR: Do you think this [reluctance on the part of audiences and financiers] is only about the international profile of the kinds of movies you show? Because on the one hand, there are the international films – the world cinema – that you're bringing. But wasn't the other main point of the AIFF to be a forum for independent filmmakers *in* India?

AS: That's true – all the film festivals are trying to support independent Indian cinema. Actually that's the only way for a film festival to try to create an identity. Otherwise if they also show Bollywood films, there is no difference between Bollywood and the film festival. So film festivals don't even have an option but to support independent cinema. Because if you don't [support it], then how do you sell it [the festival]? [laughs]. Independent films and international films are only areas where film festivals can enter the market. That's the only way film festivals can pitch the product as 'different' to financiers. We say to them, 'People will come and watch these films and the media will talk about it, and your brand will get visibility in the media.'

PR: What did you have to do in order to get the news media to pay attention to the AIFF? Did you have to get celebrities involved?

AS: I think media in India is already interested in film festivals. India is going through a transformation in the cities. Globalization has come so far and the media are by and large the most aware people in society. They know what we lack – infrastructure, good education, and cultural activities. So whenever something like a film festival comes, the media is the first organization to support it. They want to catch on to and promote anything that they see as a sign of 'changing India.' So it's not only about film festivals. If there's a new flyover, there's news about it in the papers and on TV. If a Metro system is built, they talk about that. Now in Ahmedabad, they have built a Rapid Transit System bus – it's a mass transport system; there's a special lane on the road only for these buses. It started functioning this month. This is something new that will [hopefully] improve the infrastructure and this is a sign of so-called 'Rising India.' You know? The media is hungry for this kind of news.

PR: There's also the issue of cultural nationalism when it comes to the news media.

AS: There's definitely a pervasive feeling of nationalism at the moment – it's a wave of nationalism.

PR: But it's a weird nationalism, because it's a nationalism that wants to recreate India in the image of other 'global' cities, countries.

AS: Everybody wants to make India look like Europe.

PR: Or Shanghai.

AS: So film festivals are also part and parcel of this whole scheme. Of making India look like a truly international country.

PR: What role does independent Indian cinema play in this project of building an 'international' or 'global' image for India?

AS: It's the awareness. When I speak with a German, I find he has traveled to almost every country in the world. He also knows about Japanese cinema, Korean cinema, Iranian cinema...

PR: So the logic of placing contemporary independent Indian films alongside contemporary world cinema would be to foster a sense that India is at par with these other 'global cultures' of filmmaking?

AS: Yes, that's the intention behind showing international films. But with independent Indian films, it's more about supporting the underdog. It's about saying, 'There's Bollywood, and that's fine. But there's also this independent film scene that's devoted to covering social issues, looking at life in detail, and bringing stories which are not from the metros, but say stories of poor people, the story of a Marathi person, a story from Kerala, a story from the slums ... this sort of thing.'

PR: Would you say the impulse toward this kind of independent scene is also about a similar desire for eclecticism as that which motivates the desire for the 'international'? The desire for the different, the marginal, for what's outside the norm?

AS: Yes. But that [impulse] is slightly different from festival to festival. For instance in the MIFF, there's an aura of activism. They select mostly documentaries and social subject films. But when it comes to Osian's or even AIFF, the focus is more on storytelling from the fringes of society. Not necessarily activist/social oriented stories, but nevertheless filling a gap that Bollywood isn't interested in. Honestly, I don't think there is much exciting cinema coming out of India ... and I think film festivals can make Indian cinema more exciting.

PR: Who are the key players when it comes to festivals?

AS: Kerala film festival is really big, there's one in Chennai, there are 2–3 established festivals in Calcutta. There are many in Delhi – Osian's, Vatavaran Environment and Wildlife Film festival. There are many famous ones in Bombay too.

PR: Do you distinguish between film festivals and film series like Vikalp?

AS: There's a big difference. Film series are mostly based in activism, I feel, most of the time. Vikalp for instance is more of an effort to change society, and show documentary films that are very critical of various social issues. Shamiana is focused only on short films. And then the other big difference is that the audiences for film series are small and contained. And it happens almost every month. In contrast, film festivals happen once a year, they're competitive, and bring films that don't necessarily focus on social issues, but other aspects of life too. Film festivals also bring filmmakers and the audience together. Film societies do that too, at some level, but film festivals play the role of trying to make a transactional link between independent cinema and the market, the distributors. So film festivals are trying to become a sort of market for independent cinema, which film societies and series cannot be. Osian's, IFFI are now trying to follow the model of Cannes or Sundance by integrating a film market into their structure.

PR: Was AIFF trying to follow this model too, by setting up an Independent Film Bazaar?

AS: Yes, but we were very unsuccessful in our first year! [laughs].

PR: Why do you say so?

AS: It didn't work – it was bound not to work. Because you need to have worked out so many logistics, and to have *networked* so much before you even think of mounting a film market. So you can't just think you want to do a film market and make it happen, just like that. It takes years of work. Osian's has been doing it for years and it's still not successful. IFFI's film market too, even after 14 years of experience, is still not a great success. Even that is just a beginning – it will take another 5–10 years before such film markets can become successful in India.

PR: Why do you think it's not catching on?

AS: Because there is no market for independent cinema in India. The distributors are still the same folks who have been in the film industry for the past 40–50 years and their mindset is very different. They think that in order to sell, films need to have songs, good music, stars, dancing, and all that. It's not easy to change that mindset.

PR: Do you think that the film festival has a potential to play a role in changing that? What needs to happen? Or let me rephrase that – in order to create a market for selling independent cinema, don't we need a culture of independent filmmaking and viewing first? Does the film festival play a role in that process?

AS: It should go both ways, but unfortunately at the moment it's a one-way street. We have more and more film festivals, but less good cinema. There are so many film festivals in India now, but not so much good cinema.

PR: What do you mean by good cinema?

AS: I've been watching a lot of films from Bengal, Kerala, and Tamil Nadu recently. And it's always the same story – if the script is good, then the production values are really bad. If the production quality and the script are both good, the acting is really bad. So there is always something missing in our cinema. On top of that, other world cinemas, international film cultures, have the name of a master attached to them. For instance, for Chinese cinema or Hong Kong cinema, you have Wong Kar-Wai. For Japanese cinema you have a Takeshi Kitano or a Takashi Miike. So also for Korean cinema's Park Chan-Wook. And Iran's Mohsen Makhmalbaf and Abbas Kiarostami, so many masters. Now tell me, when I say Indian cinema, do any masters come to mind?

PR: Yes, but they're all in the past! Satyajit Ray, Ritwik Ghatak, even Guru Dutt – there are several from an earlier era.

AS: Nobody recent! It's really ironic – I don't know why it's happening, but it's just a fact. So this is a big problem with Indian cinema at the moment.

PR: Is that what's making it difficult to brand independent Indian cinema – that there are no 'masters'?

AS: Yes, certainly, in my opinion.

PR: One thing I noticed which really made the film festival suffer in Ahmedabad – and this is the case not just with AIFF but also Osian's and IFFI – is that there's a Bollywood celebrity presence both on the jury and among the compères who conduct the proceedings. This makes the atmosphere *filmi* in a way that seems contrary to the aims of the film festival, and blocks dialog from happening. Can you comment on this phenomenon?

AS: I am conflicted on this point, really. I'm not able to form a point of view on whether or not the celebrity presence is a good thing. If you look at the Cannes Film Festival, the media in India and the international media in general cover it because of the red carpet. Celebrities from all around the world come to Cannes. And still Cannes manages to screen the most experimental cinema. So they are able to create a buzz *and* maintain an independent film culture.

PR: But then in Cannes, all of the non-mainstream film gets relegated to the sidebars. Isn't it widely regarded that Cannes is focused more on the mainstream market while smaller scale, lower-tier – but still quite big –

festivals like Telluride, or the Vancouver Film Festival, or the Buenos Aires International Film Festival are really more adventurous/experimental in their programming?

AS: But as one of the biggest film festivals in the world, Cannes is doing quite a decent job. Even if it doesn't fully support new independent cinema, at least it promotes the work of established off-beat directors. Berlinale recently invited Shah Rukh Khan to attend the festival, and I think that his presence there was really important in terms of generating the international audience's interest in Indian cinema. Similarly, people in India have their guard up about 'boring' world cinema or art cinema. They also assume independent cinema will be 'boring.' Celebrities are helpful in luring people to a film festival, in lowering their defenses. At the same time, there is definitely the risk that the event will become about them, and the focus will shift to the celebrities. So as I said before, I am on the fence on the issue of celebrities.

PR: What do you think is the role of the programmer/curator in a film festival?

AS: It should be just curating the films and not handling all the other details. [laughs]. But that's not how it worked out with AIFF! I don't even consider myself a good curator because I don't have the experience and skill required to be a festival curator. I should not have been asked to do this job – but unfortunately there was simply no one qualified for it in Ahmedabad at the time. In general, my feeling is that we don't have good curators in India. Those who do it tend to be really biased about one kind of cinema. So there is no sense of balance. That's the first thing that you require for a film festival to work – a good balance of films: heavy films, light films, comedies, action, social issue. There should be a mix of interesting themes and styles too. Curating films is very similar to organizing an art exhibition. The curator needs to be really aware of the history of cinema, the theory of cinema, and what's happening in the contemporary world of cinema. S/he needs to be able to articulate – or at least sense – what makes a particular film or set of films special. I have no clue about all this!

PR: Perhaps it's naïve to think that a festival curator should only be cognizant of films on the aesthetic and thematic level. A curator also needs to be an entrepreneur nowadays – Neville Tulli [director of Osian's Cinefan] is an excellent illustration of this. Part of the job is having to network with buyers, sellers, sales agents. Someone once told me it's not about which film you want for the festival, but which film you're *allowed* to get, since sales agents obviously want their films to premier at the most high-profile, top-tier festivals.

AS: Yes, it's very true that the less glamorous aspect of the curator's job is to build a network, build good relations among film festivals, other curators, filmmakers, distributors, and the audience. The other thing is that nobody understands what this job entails, especially within the organizational team – I don't think people appreciate what a delicate and tough job it is to curate films. The thing with curating is that everybody believes they can do it. Their mindset is like this: 'We have 20 films, we'll divide them up into groups according to the available time, and screen them! It's that simple!' But of course good film festivals don't work like that. I hope that with emerging film festivals, good curators will also be nurtured in India.

PR: One other difference between the film festival v. film series issue you mentioned before is that film series are based around creating viewing communities – communities that care about and have a stake in what films do and how they work in society, and film festivals by and large back away from that task. The focus of film festivals tends to be less on the *relation* between the audience and the film and more on films themselves. So the film becomes a god you go worship in a dark place, cut off from the rest of the world!

AS: The other difference between the two is that film series screen very interesting films and a lot of interaction happens. But the film festival – and this isn't yet happening in India at the scale at which it's happening elsewhere – is the only space where the *development* of cinema can be discussed among filmmakers, critics, and the audience. The flipside of this is that sometimes films are revered only for their form, not their content.

PR: What I'm hearing you say is that film festivals are a unique medium in that a large and varied group of actors (filmmakers, critics, the media, spectators, distributors, sales agents) assemble together. But do they really talk to each other, much less discuss the developmental issues in cinema?

AS: In AIFF it didn't happen, but in IFFI it happens to some extent, and in Osian's it happens nicely sometimes. They have special discussion forums, panels, roundtables and seminars with experts themed around various topics. And I'm sure you've been to international film festivals where it happens a lot.

PR: What's interesting to me is how film festivals shape, limit, and structure the kinds of interactions, conversations, and transactions that can take place. There seems to be a sense that film festivals are spaces totally 'open' for all kinds of encounters, but even those spaces which imagine themselves as being an agora of sorts are 'closed' in ways that would be very interesting to discuss. I'm thinking for instance of the Flaherty Film Seminar that's held in New York every year, and features the work of emerging filmmakers alongside more canonical works. The program is not publicized beforehand, so there is the conceit of 'non-preconception,' or the idea that the audience should experience the film in a state of total innocence. Each screening is followed by an hour-long discussion. So the Flaherty Seminar is not a traditional 'film festival,' but since it is attended by several well-regarded programmers and distributors – albeit in their 'private' personas and not in their official capacity – it is definitely a forum through which relatively unknown work gains in both cultural and economic capital. And even in this setting – of a week-long immersive 'camp' for adults, which allows for deep-interaction, and immersing yourself in not only the films but in the group of people – the structuring of the event and of the long-form audience discussions is such that conversations/interactions settle into predictable and problematic patterns.

AS: My experience is that film festivals are not a platform where you start a discussion and reach its conclusion. You can almost compare film festival discussions to the discussions of global warming at the international level – be it in the news media or in more casual or critical settings. A lot of talk, a lot of projections, blueprints, what to do in the next 30 years – but in the end, nothing happens. [laughs].

PR: Can you talk a little bit about your experience at any recent festivals abroad that you have attended, and say something about what 'worked' and why?

AS: I recently attended the Munich Film Festival – the way Munich is structured, you take part in some discussions, and nothing happens in those discussions themselves, but you always end up meeting good people who have the same sort of point of view, or a similar interest in cinema, and sometimes you stay in touch with them. I stayed in touch with a few people from Munich, and we met again in Cologne and Berlin to talk about cinema – and in the future we might be making a film together. So in that way, such a film festival connects like-minded people and helps to foster the making of a certain kind of cinema – a synergy – which might never have come into the world without this platform.

PR: So the film festival can be a networking space, a space where future conversations and projects get started.

AS: Yes.

PR: What needs to be put in place in order for that to happen in India? Or maybe: What about that model would you change? Does the fact that we're just getting started in India make it a good setting for experiments?

AS: I'll answer the first question! [laughs]. The second one is harder. I think in order for it to happen in India.... Let me put it this way: the biggest problem in India at the moment – with any form of art – is that in India if you go with your work to someone, be it photography, or painting, or film, or poetry, or literature, or art, or whatever ... your work doesn't matter so much. What always matters is *who sent you*. Or which family you belong to, or whom do you know. This needs to change first.

PR: Would you say that this kind of nepotistic, or aristocratic, or 'old boys network' structure of society, rather than a meritocracy, is bad for art and politics?

AS: Yes. What I see around me all the time is that there are so many good artists who don't have good networks – they don't come from wealthy families or intellectual families. And they don't know anyone. And nobody asks them to show their work. So what happens when they reach near 30 is that they realize that they've been focusing on improving their skill or their art or their craft, on immersing themselves in the process of creating something beautiful. But those other people who invested 10 years in networking are the ones who get much further ahead of them. When they look at their work and compare it to those people who invested time in networking instead of art, they realize they are doing better work, but nobody knows about them. And this realization breaks the spirit of most independent filmmakers and independent artists.

PR: Do you feel the situation of film festivals elsewhere, say Munich, is something to aspire to in this regard?

AS: I don't think things are perfect in Europe or in the US – I think there too everything hinges on networking and whom you know. But at least because of grants and institutional support, funding, and sponsorship, if you are doing good work – even if you are 'no one' – you can get a small amount of recognition. You don't have to struggle for 20 years. In India, this period of struggle [for artists who don't start out rich] is just too long. There are simply no grants. That needs to change if we want to change something about Indian cinema. I don't know how, but we have so many internationally acclaimed filmmakers now: Shekhar Kapur, Mira Nair, Deepa Mehta. What are they doing for Indian cinema?

PR: Do you think these diasporic filmmakers are interested in doing anything explicitly 'for' non-Bollywood Indian cinema beyond 'branding' it?

AS: If I were in their position I would try to do more – I would try to create some sort of support system for people who don't start out having one, who aren't already connected. Like Berlinale's 'Talent Campus' [a six-day symposium retreat for emerging filmmakers including discussions, workshops, and lectures with industry professionals]. It can take different forms – I can't tell you what can be done [laughs]. But there are already so many models in the world that you can take. You can make a lottery fund. You can take 5% of your film's profit and put it into a lottery fund, and finance the film of a first-time director who has made a nice short film.

PR: Given that you are a filmmaker yourself, do you think festival directors and programmers have a responsibility too, in terms of fostering particular kinds of relationships between filmmakers and the audience, and funders/distributors?

AS: Yes. Film festivals need to provide a forum for conversation about the films – so I think Q&A or discussions after films are important. But first, they need to take on the role of educating people about the history of cinema. So that audiences can actually appreciate something that is new and experimental, where the director has tried to break rules and norms to make something wonderful. But that can happen only after years of watching films, no? Not just after one night of watching films. And in India you can't be overly optimistic about people suddenly being able to appreciate what is good and bad cinema. You also need to keep this in mind – that this is something new that is happening in cinema. It's going to take time. You can't be so aggressive, and ask, 'Why are you not able to tell that this is good cinema? Why are you not asking questions?' They're not used to it. Films in India are something that people go to watch either with their

| | families – where you can eat popcorn and laugh – or that they go to watch on television or in a theater because they're tired with the day's work, and they want to escape somewhere. These are the only two reasons to watch film in India, so you can't expect these people to suddenly go and start discussing cinema. It's not going to happen easily – it will take years. |

PR: So what you're saying is that film festivals have the capacity to produce a change in people's relationship to cinema in India – but that this cannot happen in a vacuum, a whole infrastructure is needed to make this happen.

AS: Absolutely, absolutely. It needs to happen at the level of schools. In Europe and US, film studies is a part of the curriculum, and film societies are active in schools and colleges, where films are shown, discussed, and experts are called in to talk with students. We don't have all that.

PR: To end, what did people tell you about the AIFF when you returned after it ended? [Singh had to leave AIFF on its very first day to attend the Munich Film Festival]

AS: Everybody is annoyed, everybody. No one who worked for the film festival is happy. I didn't meet a single person who said they were really happy after working with the film festival.

PR: Why do you think this was so?

AS: Because everything was so chaotic, so disorganized, so manipulative, that people got tired. But then the nice thing is that the best thing Dorothy [Dorothy Wenner – Berlinale curator who attended AIFF as a Jury member] said when I met her in Paris: she said that only after doing the first version of a film festival does one learn how to do a film festival. [laughs]. So the next time it will be much better. Because there are just so many parameters that you just aren't aware of before doing it. It really looks easy to do it on paper. It looks even easier after downloading the BFI guidebook on 'How to set up a Film Festival.' We all read it and thought, 'We can do it!' Now we *actually* know how to do it.

PR: What did you feel about the Jury selections for winners?

AS: I didn't like any of them [laughs].

PR: After the jury announcements were made, some of us drove back to the hotel with Kajal Ojha, one of the jurors. She was talking about the winner of the short film category, '88 Keys to Happiness,' and asked us repeatedly if we had seen this 'great film.' We told her we had found the film very melodramatic, and that it was a bit like a cross between a Bollywood film and a Hallmark commercial. Her response was: 'But it is an *Indian* film! That's why it won.' It was interesting – and a bit depressing – to hear that (a) independent films from India are judged based on whether they convey

	an essence of Indianness and that (b) Indianness = melodrama + sentimentality + an aesthetic of commerciality.
AS:	[laughs] We don't have good curators or adequate jury members.
PR:	Will do you the festival again next year?
AS:	I would participate again if I was asked to. Everybody put a lot of work into it, and at the end, even though there is a lot of bitterness all around, some things are bigger than personal ambition or hurt. So putting those feelings aside, I'd do it again.... The first thing we'd change is to eliminate the market – the Independent Film Bazaar. And second, we'll do it at a smaller scale, and focus on the films.

Note

1. http://parotechnics.blogspot.com.

Notes on contributor

Pooja Rangan is a Ph.D. candidate in the Department of Modern Culture and Media at Brown University. She has a background in documentary filmmaking, which she now combines with her interest in biopolitics, ethnography, and technicity. Her doctoral dissertation, titled 'Automatic Ethnography: Otherness, Indexicality, and "New" Visual Media,' investigates the emergence and persistence of autoethnography, as a visual technology for governing beleaguered social subjects (the subaltern, the indigenous native, the child, the animal, the refugee), and as an idiom that illustrates the limits of contemporary speculative models of politics. Rangan's work has been published in the *SARAI Reader* and is forthcoming in *Camera Obscura* and the *Oxford Guide to Postcolonial Studies*.

References

Bazin, Andre. "The Film Festival Viewed as a Religious Order." *Dekalog 3: On Film Festivals*. Trans. Emilie Bickerton. Ed. Richard Porton. London: Wallflower Press, 2009. 13–19. Print.
Benjamin, Walter. "The Work of Art in the Age of Mechanical Reproduction." *Illuminations*. Trans. Harry Zohn. New York: Schocken Books, 1968. 217–52. Print.
Dayan, Daniel. "Looking for Sundance: The Social Construction of a Film Festival." *Moving Images, Culture, and the Mind*. Ed. Ib Bondebjerg. London: U of Luton P, 2000. 43–52. Print.
De Valck, Marijke. *Film Festivals: From European Geopolitics to Global Cinephilia*. Amsterdam: U of Amsterdam P, 2007. Print.
Krauss, Rosalind. "The Cultural Logic of the Late Capitalist Museum." *October* 54 (Autumn 1990): 3–17. Print.
O'Doherty, Brian. *Inside the White Cube: The Ideology of the Gallery Space*. Berkeley: U of California P, 1986. Print.
Porton, Richard. "Introduction: On Film Festivals." *Dekalog 3: On Film Festivals*. Ed. Richard Porton. London: Wallflower Press, 2009. 1–10. Print.
Prasad, Madhava. "This Thing Called Bollywood." *Seminar Web Edition*, No. 525 (May 2003). Web. 25 Oct. 2009. <http://www.india-seminar.com/semsearch.htm>.
Putnam, James. *Art and Artifact: The Museum as Medium*. London: Thames and Hudson, 2001. Print.
Rajadhyaksha, Ashish. "The Bollywoodization of Indian Cinema: Cultural Nationalism in a Global Arena." *Inter-Asia Cultural Studies* 4.1 (2003): 25–39. Print.
Turan, Kenneth. *Sundance to Sarajevo: Film Festivals and the World They Make*. Berkeley: U of California P, 2002. Print.

Vasudevan, Ravi. "Addressing the Spectator of a 'Third World' National Cinema: The Bombay 'Social' Film of the 1940s and 1950s." *Screen* 36.4 (1995): 305–24. Print.

Indian film festivals cited

Ahmedabad International Film Festival: <http://aifilmfest.com/> [expired link]; <http://www.fulmarxx.net/index.php?option=com_content&task=view&id=14&Itemid=27>.
Chennai Film Festival: <http://www.chennaifilmfest.org/>.
Experimenta, The International Festival for Experimental Cinema in India: No current website; For information on founder Shai Heredia, see: <http://www.indiaifa.org/stafftrusteearticle.asp?id=214&inputtypebreadcrumb=staff&tablename=team>.
International Film Festival of India [IFFI aka Goa International Film Festival]: <http://iffi.gov.in/>.
Kerala Film Festival: <http://www.keralafilm.com/>.
Kolkata Film Festival: <http://www.kff.in/>.
Madurai Film Festival: <http://www.maduraifilmfest.blogspot.com/>.
Mocha Film Club: <http://www.mocha.co.in/filmclub.html>.
Monsoon Film Festival: <http://www.themonsoonfestival.com/>.
Mumbai International Film Festival [MIFF]: <http://www.miffindia.in/>.
Osian's Cinefan: <http://www.osians.com/cinefan.html>, <http://64.38.56.174/index.html>.
Persistence Resistance/Magic Lantern Foundation: <http://www.magiclanternfoundation.org/PersistenceFest/PR_Mainpage.html>.
Pune International Film Festival: <http://www.puneinternationalfilmfestival.com/.
Shamiana Short Film Club: <http://shamiana-theshortfilmclub.blogspot.com/>.
Vatavaran Environmental and Wildlife Film Festival: <http://cmsvatavaran.org/>.
Vikalp Film Series: <http://www.freedomfilmsindia.org/>.

Confessions of the (ethnic) narcissist: Intermedia in diaspora

Ani Maitra

Department of Modern Culture and Media, Brown University, Providence, USA

> This essay attempts to examine the ethico-political implications of 'ethnic narcissism' through an analysis of Harjant Gill's video *Milind Soman Made Me Gay* (2007). Drawing on Rey Chow's theorization of the ethnic writer's autobiographical turn in diaspora and to psychoanalytic theories of narcissism, the essay plays close attention to Gill's use of intermediality to think through a queer diasporic politics that both deploys and undoes identity politics. If homosexuality (and narcissism) continues to be racialized in certain forms of nationalist discourse in the US, the essay suggests that we look at Gill's narcissistic, queer performance as something that makes possible an ethnically aware self-expression as well as the articulation of the failure of an 'authentic' ethnic identity.

What precisely is the status of authors writing about themselves-always-deemed-to-be-writing-about-themselves anyway? How would post-structuralist theory respond to this border – between transindividual narcissistic attachment and persistent social dismissal – along which the ethnic is destined to pick up the scraps of her psychic economy? However migratory, hybridized, and in flux it might be, is not ethnicity in this context finally assigned the value of a referent that confines and immobilizes? (Chow 152)

Care of the self does not entail locating the truth of the self. In this view, the other may be seen not as a threatening source of alien enigmas, but rather as that with which one can have less antagonistic kinds of relationship. The other would remain other without having to be either reassuringly identical to oneself or markedly different. (Dean 121)

Intermedia is not only ineffable. It is inherently confronting: producing new thoughts, processes, forms that are not predictable; mongrels which defy categorization; sexualities which challenge the status quo hard to define, defiant. (Breder 214)

Introduction

If the psychoanalytic categories of melancholia and hysteria have been challenged by literary criticism to account for the specificity of the marginalized subjectivity of the post-colonial and/or diasporic subject,[1] narcissism continues to be deemed a condition that is egotistic, entrapping and best avoided.[2] A telling example of the continuing pathologization of narcissism in popular discourse would be spy novelist John LeCarré's remark in *The Nation* soon after the 9/11 attacks. LeCarré describes Osama bin Laden as a 'man of narcissistic homoeroticism,' who would also herald his own undoing since 'his barely containable male vanity, his appetite for self-drama and his closet passion for limelight ... would be his downfall, seducing him into a final dramatic act of self-destruction, produced, directed, scripted and acted to death by Osama bin Laden himself" (LeCarré 15–17). LeCarré's reference to narcissism is intriguing for a number of reasons: first, because it projects homophobia on to the body of the terrorist and racial other;[3] second, because it evokes the theatricality of a 'scenario' where bin Laden, as the narcissistic artist scripts and performs a drama of death-dealing self-recognition; and third, because LeCarré's homosexualization of the racial other is also an inversion of Freud's own displacement of racial difference on to his account of homosexual narcissism. If the pathologization of narcissism – from Freud to LeCarré – reveals the ways in which homophobia and racism are consistently combined in discursive formations, this paper attempts a queer-diasporic (counter)reading of narcissistic performance in Harjant Gill's *Milind Soman Made Me Gay*. Gill's video, I argue, uses elements of 'intermedia' to complicate what Rey Chow calls the 'coercive mimeticism' of ethnic minorities in diaspora. Gill's homotextuality, I suggest, is inseparable from a narcissistic performance that is not merely confined to the ethnic self but rather impinged upon and shaped by varying forms of racial and sexual otherness. In the first section of the essay, I draw upon Chow's work to chart the connections between the minority ethnic writer's (invariably) 'autobiographical' turn and theories of narcissism. I then attempt to reconfigure Chow's conclusions about immigrant writing in the context of Gill's video: I pay close attention to the artist's use of intermediality to suggest that, here, the ethnic body is narcissistic *in order to be* an archive for a queer history, and to challenge notions of sequence and development. I consistently focus on the intermedial, performative dimensions (and therefore the effects of 'performativity') of narcissism in the text. The final section of the paper pushes its reflexivity further in that it attempts to read itineraries that remain 'outside' Gill's frame of representation: ethnic identity, class, and gender are three categories that I bring up in the context of queer-diasporic cultural production to suggest that the video itself announces a certain awareness of what it 'fails' to represent.

Coercive mimeticism and the autobiography in diaspora

In her book *The Protestant Ethnic and the Spirit of Capitalism*, Rey Chow observes that there are at least *three* imbricated levels of 'mimeticism' or 'imitation' that operate in contexts of cross-cultural representation. The first level, which is really a legacy of colonial encounters, takes the white man as the irreplaceable 'original.' This form of imitation, Chow suggests, compels the non-white mimic to be always an 'inferior' copy. The second level of mimeticism is a more complex version of the first in that it claims to disturb the self/other and the colonizer/colonized binaries. This level focuses on the psyche, indeterminacy, and ambivalence of the colonized subject; and aims to grant her a certain amount of 'agency' and 'selfhood.'[4] What interests me, however, is the *third* level of mimeticism that Chow defines in terms of 'ethnic' self-assertion.[5] She calls this mode of representation 'coercive mimeticism':

> ... the level at which the ethnic person is expected to come to resemble what is recognizably ethnic. This is also the level at which the intimate mutual implications between mimeticism and visuality need yet again to be foregrounded, albeit in a different manner. What makes this third kind of mimeticism intriguing is that the original that is supposed to be replicated is no longer the white man or his culture but rather an image, a stereotyped view of the ethnic: I am referring to the 'Asianness,' 'Africanness,' 'Arabness,' and other similar kinds of nativenesses with which ethnics in North American society are often expected to conform. (Chow 107)

For Chow, the idea of 'coercive mimeticism' is inseparable from Louis Althusser's description of 'interpellation,' where the various apparatuses of civil society 'hail' the individual to constitute herself as a 'subject.' However, coercive mimeticism, she further argues, easily slides towards an *explicitly* confessional mode, a 'turn toward the self, especially the ethnic self – as a form of production' (Chow 111). In connection with this (auto)biographical tendency in immigrant writing, Chow draws upon and moves beyond Freud's psychoanalytic notion of narcissism, gesturing towards the need for a clearer understanding of the relationship between the psychic and the social in the context of diasporic and minority ethnic representation. In this argument, the ethnic self appears 'narcissistic' precisely because her narcissism has been disallowed by racial and cultural hegemony, her image remaining largely 'unmirrored' in the social speculum, even as she is repeatedly summoned to mimic her own ethnicity. Recast in terms of the social, the affect of ethnic narcissism thus becomes a 'symptom' of marginalization and repression, of narcissism of the dominant ideology. This (repressed or thwarted) collective narcissism, however, is not narcissistic in the popular sense (of self-absorption, solipsism etc.) in that it actually goes *beyond the individual*, since it mediates between the individual ethnic artist and the ethnic *community*. It is this oscillation that could potentially transform narcissism into a 'transindividual issue of attachment and belonging.' Yet paradoxically, even as it gestures towards a larger community, transindividual narcissism is irreducible to a single, unique identity. Chow writes:

> How is the experience of an inaccessible narcissism to be represented? How can something that has not, as it were, been allowed to develop, and is therefore not empirically available, be written about? It is at the limit of what is representable – of the need to write about something whose existence has nonetheless been placed out of reach – that the tendency to be autobiographical among immigrant writers takes on special significance. For, seen in this light, autobiographical writing is perhaps not simply a straightforward account of oneself but more a symptomatic attempt (born of coercive mimeticism and social interpellation to be sure) to create access to a transindividual narcissism – to grope for a 'self-regard' that does not yet exist.... Moreover, might not access to such self-regard, however remote in the present, promise, in the end, to vindicate the group's identity – the elusive yet undeniable something called 'Asian Americanness'? (Chow 142)

In other words, transindividual narcissism, potentially, could offer a way *out of* the imperative prescriptions of interpellation and coercive mimeticism. That is to say, it could radically alter the notion of the self and the relationship between the self and the larger community. However, Chow herself is sceptical of this *theoretical* possibility, and makes a general distinction between post-structuralist theorization on the one hand, and *non-theoretical* 'autobiographical speaking and writing' on the other hand. Analysing personal essays collected in the anthology *Under Western Eyes*,[6] she emphasizes the sheer sense of 'abjection,' 'entrapment' and 'haunting' that marks ethnic self-expression:

> Contrary to poststructuralist theorists of hybridity, the writers of these personal essays, all of which are about the experience of actually living as cultural hybrids, offer pictures that are anything but freedom from the given. Instead, hybridity itself, as the cultural given, becomes for these ethnically marked writers a form of existential entrapment ... an oppressive condition that does not automatically improve with its representation and confession in writing. The act of writing autobiographically in these pieces is much more than being selfish; it is simultaneously writing collectively about the inherited, *shared* condition of social stigmatization and abjection. (Chow 146)

In other words, 'narcissism,' 'autobiography' and 'ethnicity' have little to offer to Hongo's selection of immigrant writers seeking liberation from the marginalized subjectivity imposed on them. While the aim of my essay is not to dispute Chow's reading of the writers in Hongo's collection, I want to take up her general distinction between *theoretical* and *non-theoretical* writing through my reading of ethnic self-expression in a different socio-cultural (con)text. Specifically, I want to read Gill's narcissistic video as a kind of 'writing' that problematizes the disjunction that Chow sees between the anticipatory, 'futuristic' temporality of theory on the one hand, and the 'backward' glance of autobiographical writing and fiction on the other. I will suggest that the video allows itself to be read as something *in-between*, or as an *intermediary* that constantly negotiates between these two poles of prescriptive theory and 'creative writing,' of the future and the past. In that sense, what follows will try to map the political affinities between intermediate states, or rather structures and affects of in-betweeness: diaspora, narcissism and intermedia.

However, before I turn to the video and its formal characteristics, I want to bring Chow's discussion of coercive mimeticism in dialogue with contemporary queer theory. It is important to note that 'repetition' plays a key role in Chow's theorization of performance of ethnicity and the formation of an ethnicized subjectivity: 'In order to be, this ethnic must both be seen to own her ethnicity and to exhibit it repeatedly. This repeated exhibition nowadays takes to tend the form of confession, an act that, in the terms of this discussion, may be renamed *self-mimicry*' (Chow 112). Here, it will be useful to trace plausible connections between interpellation, ethnic performance and performativity. I am specifically referring to the work of Judith Butler and Eve Kosofsky Sedgwick, both of whom investigate the possibility of 'perversions' of performative utterances interpellating the hailed subject. In spite of the differences in their approach, both Butler and Sedgwick agree that performatives are turned into 'deformatives' by the 'torque' imparted by queerness.[7] Performativity, in queer theory, thus becomes the bearer of a radical 'excess' and designates the *potential* to deflect the subject's response to a performative into something it did not originally set out to be. Butlerian performativity insists on decentring identity of the performing 'I,' not to disavow the political necessity of identity politics, but to open up queerness itself to possibilities of re-signification and re-inscription.[8]

Although Chow does not draw upon the notion of queer performativity, it is possible to argue that transindividual narcissism would also lend itself to performativity and stage *repetitive and hence sometimes dissonant* performances of ethnicity. That is to say, if we see coercive mimeticism through queer performativity – as *performances (sometimes not) responding to performatives* – transindividual narcissism could also be seen to decentre identity of the ethnic 'I.' Narcissism, here, could facilitate a movement not just beyond the *self* but perhaps even outside that specific *ethnic* formation that the bio-political processes of interpellation demand of the subject.[9] I do not mean to suggest that these performances suggest an unproblematic 'agency' of the ethnic self. That is to say, this movement of the ethnic subject beyond ethnicity, we might continue to maintain, is as unintended and uncontrollable as it is in Butler's definition of performativity.[10] I have a different set of questions from my reading of Chow and Butler: What might diaspora and queer theory learn from a *non-heteronormative* remediation of ethnic narcissism? Can ethnic narcissism as a mimetic and performative mode be *read* differently in a queer-diasporic context, precisely because psychoanalytic theory has associated narcissism not just with art and literature but also with racial otherness and homosexuality? How do I, as someone who studies diaspora/media theory and practice, *ethically* revisit 'narcissism' as well as the theory-practice dialectic (as opposed to a strict binary) when I chance upon an instance of queer performativity that *fails* to secure the limits of ethnic identity? I raise these issues because they seem extremely relevant to me in the context of Gill's video that – as I will go on to argue – heavily relies on the notion of performing an identity that, at once, *is and is not* 'gay' and 'South Asian.' And I attempt to answer the questions posed above by delineating a queer-diasporic *reading practice*: I suggest that the political contours of this reading practice – the productive and non-pathological connections between narcissism, homosexuality, and race in diaspora – come into being in this encounter, in an intermedial middle space, between textuality on the one hand and theoretical reflexivity on the other.

Milind Soman Made Me Gay: 'outing' the intermedial and ethnic narcissus

Assuming that most readers have not seen *Milind Soman Made Me Gay*, I will begin this section by summarizing the trajectory of the video, primarily to give them a sense of the flow of the 'narrative' and the structure of the piece. In a few broad strokes, I will also sketch how Gill positions himself in a piece that I am calling 'intermedial,' and in between histories that are apparently not contiguous.

Intermedia, a concept formulated by German artist Hans Breder in the 1960s, is interested in producing *frictions* between different media like film, theatre, music, poetry, and the visual arts. In their performances and installations, Breder and his followers aim not so much to 'fuse' or 'unite' disparate media (which would make their work closer to 'multimedia' and 'mixed media'), but rather to emphasize the interaction and encounter between the disparities, and transform the structure of each medium.[11] Breder's 'Mass in A-Minor for Suitcases' (see Figure 3) is often cited as an unruly hybrid performance that most explicitly announces itself as intermedia. 'Mass in A-Minor,' intermedia critics suggest, attempts to open up a 'mongrel' communication space between media by juxtaposing the architecture of the Bremen Cathedral, original music and chanting, video images of human displacements and suffering, images of textual fragments (like the Declaration of the Rights of Man) and theatrical movement by an actor. Intermedia theorist David E. Klemm writes: 'The Mass in A-Minor for Suitcases is intermedia on a grand scale – and its success is to create a space of alchemical transformation. ... Here the intermedial element works at the level of conflict of interpretations' (Klemm 68–69). Klemm and others emphasize the installation's or performance's capacity to create a zone of exchange, not just between the media used, but also between the 'performance' of visual and aural signifiers and the participating viewer (see Spielmann 133). Intermedia, then, by its very nature, is analogous to a Barthesian 'text' that foregrounds a critical and theoretical reflexivity. For Klemm, an intermedia performance compels the viewer to perform a 'mediating' role to make sense of what is unfolding on in front of her eyes:

> The 'I' of mediating, the intermedial 'I' is a second-order, reflexive 'I' – a pure activity of relating 'between' the primary subjectivity and the concrete one here and now. In other words, 'I' divide between primary subjectivity that relates to this one here, and a second-order subjectivity that relates to my own relating. (Klemm 74)

I find Klemm's formulation useful because of its insistence on viewing or 'reading' intermedia as an exercise in a reflexive reading practice. As a concept, intermedia also interests me because of the critical position it takes against 'identity' or 'unity' of the mediums as well as the meanings their readings produce. Indeed, this theoretical position may also be called 'queer' in so far as it wants to both use and unsettle notions of a particular medium's identity and specificity. Such a reading of intermedia may not be farfetched given that Breder himself, reflecting on the hybridity and the anti-systemic tenor in his practice, links it to 'definitions that derive from the sexual: hermaphrodite, androgyne, bisexual' (Breder 214). More recently, José Esteban Muñoz has suggested that the intermedia process be 'seen as a radical understanding of interdisciplinarity ... in relation to both art-making protocols and taxonomies of race, gender and sex' (Muñoz 126). With these preliminary remarks on the radical potential of intermedia, let me turn to Gill's video *Milind Soman Made Me Gay*.

Figure 1. Still from *Milind Soman Made Me Gay* (2007). Directed by Harjant Gill.

Divided into a prologue and three sections, the video foregrounds Gill as his own protagonist as he recollects his past in India and then as an immigrant in the United States. His is the narrating voiceover using the autobiographical 'I'; and his is the body placed in front of a projection wall or a screen, sometimes caught in motion and sometimes still, sometimes confronting the camera and sometimes turning away to interact with the images on the screen (see Figures 1 and 2). These fragmentary performances using this conceptual interplay between various media – like archival images and video, textual fragments, music, voiceover and theatrical gestures of the silent performer – are strongly reminiscent of Breder's 'Mass in A-Minor.'

The intermittent use of intermedia elements within the piece, however, needs to be distinguished from Gill's overarching use of the medium of video, and his attempt to construct a 'narrative.' For although Gill juxtaposes his own presence against the interviews of three other men, the autobiographical element of the video (also evident from its title) cannot be missed. It is possible to argue that by repeating (the performance of) the speaking and acting 'I,' Gill demonstrates some of the narcissistic symptoms that

Figure 2. Still from *Milind Soman Made Me Gay* (2007). Directed by Harjant Gill.

Figure 3. Still from a performance of Hans Breder's 'Mass in A-Minor for Suitcases.' Germany 2000.

Chow lists in the context of immigrant writing. Indeed, the purpose of the project lies in Gill's acts of 'remembering' his past in India and in the United States; the artist-anthropologist does have trouble speaking of his Sikh 'origins'; and the idea of 'home' is also, perhaps typically, marked by an 'irresolvable ambivalence.'[12] In his prologue, for instance, Gill's voiceover informs his audience of the immediate 'event' that inspires the project – his journey 'homeward': 'I am returning to India for the first time in ten years. Every thought of going back fills me with dread. I am afraid that the place that I have called home my entire life might no longer exist. Ten years suddenly seem like a lifetime ... a lifetime of change, a lifetime of longing and a lifetime of exile.' These fears seem to come true, since the visit (and the video) ends with Gill suggesting (again, not uncommonly) that he is suspended in a 'homeless' indeterminate space: 'When I am in a room full of people, the first question that I am asked is 'Where are you from?' I no longer have an answer to that question.'

However, it is important to note that within this 'typical' framing, Gill's use of a narcissistic content and form[13] does not confine itself to either a representation of the self or of a single community. That is to say, the ethnic self speaks of 'ontological liminality'[14] not just through his own (or his community's) predicament, but also through events outside his own sexual and communal history. If the prologue speaks of Gill's desire to return home, the first section (called 'Child's Escape') turns to his experiences as a seven-year-old boy, but only to 'remember' the Hindu other in the Anti-Sikh riots in India in 1984. In the central second section (titled 'Obscene Objects and the Order of Nature' and still set in India), Gill recalls his teenage obsession with Bollywood actor/model Milind Soman, but also makes a larger connection between homophobia and moral policing, between an oppressive anti-sodomy law and an 'anti-obscenity' statute often used together by the homophobic state apparatuses in India. And the third and fourth sections of the video ('Inescapable Fate' and 'Indefinite Deferral') move to Gill's life as a queer immigrant in the US, but also juxtapose (the seemingly unrelated) homophobic killing of Matthew Shepard in Wyoming in 1998 against the racist murder of Balbir Singh Sodhi in Arizona in the aftermath of 9/11.[15]

How are we to view these connections between fragments of Gill's coercive mimeticism? Or to put it differently: what might we learn about *narcissism* from mimesis that is not only 'ethnic,' but also one that blatantly allows its *sexual* liminality to both mediate and fracture the writing of the self? On the one hand, these fragments are repetitions in so far as they are parts of Gill's continuing quest for a racio-sexual 'identity' as a Sikh, gay man in diaspora, a quest emerging from thwarted narcissism. On the other hand, the weaving together of these otherwise disconnected events or 'wounds' – each associated with some kind of psychic and/or physical violence, but not really adding up to a comprehensive 'narrative' of the ethnic self – complicates the literary/creative narcissism we have discussed so far. I am suggesting that we call this juxtaposition of disparate elements within and between the sections a performance of 'intermedial narcissism.' Before I explain what I mean, let me offer a brief summary of the psychoanalytic discourse on narcissism.

In his essay 'On Narcissism,' Freud speculates on 'primary narcissism' as a stage when the ego is formed, lying between the stages of autoerotism and object-cathexis. That is to say, we love ourselves before we learn to love others, and that (primary) narcissism is an essential but *intermediate* step for the child who will eventually learn to love others. 'Secondary narcissism,' caused by 'the drawing in of object-cathexes' into the (developed) ego, is therefore a remnant of, or a return to that primary narcissism (see Freud 'On Narcissism'). The Freud of *The Ego and the Id*, however, contradicts this model to suggest that the ego is a 'precipitate of the abandoned object-cathexes and that it contains a history of those object-choices' (Freud *Ego* 24). Here, the 'identification' of the ego-under-construction with the (lost and external) object, or the process by which the distinction between the two is lost, is, in a sense, narcissistic. Rereading Freud's theories of ego formation, Lacan famously describes the process by which the child (mis)recognizes her 'image' in 'the mirror stage' and thereby loses the distinction between herself and what is, in effect, external to her (Lacan 2). Jean Laplanche reinterprets Lacan's 'mirror' not merely as the *instrument* of reflection, but rather as the possibility of 'the recognition of the form of another human and the concomitant precipitation within the individual of a first outline of that form' (Laplanche 81). That is to say, according to Laplanche, the (narcissistic) ego can be constituted only through a recognition of the other. André Green also turns to both Freud and Lacan to emphasize the conditioning presence of the (m)other in primary or infantile narcissism. Returning to the Freud's scenario of the child at the mother's breast, Green makes the compelling argument that auto-erotism and narcissism develop at the same time that the suckling infant is trying to distinguish himself from the (m)other.[16]

I summarize these theories of ego-formation only to suggest that the notion of narcissism as a solipsistic, self-contained state is heavily contested *within* psychoanalytic theory itself. It appears that the apparently absent other is, in fact, responsible for a primary narcissistic state. Nevertheless, how do we conceptualize the other once we move beyond the theories of infantile sexuality? If narcissism (or taking oneself as the object of love in response to social interpellation) is 'more a *structure* than a state, a component of psychic life apt to manifest itself whenever the burden of desire on the subject becomes intolerable' (Cohen 42), how do we think of encounters with *racial and ethnic otherness* that is not confined to the paternal and the maternal influences on the infant?[17] Last but not least, what happens if we include homosexuality as well as racial difference as interrelated components of Freud's psycho-social elaboration of narcissism?[18] I ask these questions not to answer them by psychoanalysing Gill or his performance, but rather to reframe artistic/literary narcissism in a queer-diasporic context.

Homosexuality, after all, to return to Freud's 'On Narcissism,' is intimately connected with a narcissistic object-choice, or more specifically, the inability of the individual to abandon the 'primary narcissism' of his childhood. The (heterosexual) development of the ego, within this schema, is possible only through 'a departure from the primary narcissism.'[19] In his essay on Leonardo da Vinci, Freud writes,

> The child's love for his mother cannot continue to develop consciously any further; it succumbs to repression. The boy represses his love for his mother: he *puts himself in her place*, identifies himself with her, and takes his own person as a model in whose likeness he chooses the new object of his love. In this way he has become a homosexual. What he has in fact done is to slip back to auto-erotism.... He finds the objects of his love along the path of *narcissism*, as we say; for Narcissus, according to the Greek legend, was a youth who preferred his own reflection to everything else... (Freud 'Leonardo da Vinci' 100)

This well-known 'scenario' of male homosexual object-choice in Freud is thus one of repression, one that involves the simultaneous psychic identification with and ousting of the (m)other seen as a rival. I want to begin reading Gill's intermedial performance through a catachrestic appropriation of this scenario. The second section of the video ('Obscene Objects and the Order of Nature') opens with Gill longingly looking at the camera and caressing himself. He then turns to face and touch the 'controversial' image of Milind Soman and Madhu Sapre projected on the screen. As he confesses his adolescent sexual desire for Soman, Gill stands poised to take Sapre's place in the photograph, his body half inside and half outside a frame with the text of the anti-sodomy law of the Indian Penal Code, covering the nudity of Gill and Sapre (see Figures 4 and 5). His voiceover recalls:

> Milind Soman had these deep sunken lonely eyes. I would lose myself in them. I desired his eyes and I desired him ... I am 15 years old and I have just come across the picture.... He's holding her not to draw her near, but to maintain a safe distance from her. His eyes do not acknowledge her presence. They are lost into loneliness until I find them. *Soon I will cast her out of the picture*. It will just be me and him, left there standing, lost in each other's eyes...

Arguably, I am not suggesting that this performance be read as a parodistic, literal re-enactment of the Freudian scenario: Madhu Sapre is not Gill's 'mother,' Milind Soman not quite the 'model' (i.e. the self as a model) that Freud describes, and the actor is not fifteen years of age. It is also important to note that, unlike in the Freudian scenario, the superimposition of the three mediums here – the actor's body, the image and the text – does not represent a 'unity' of time and place: with the intermedial comes the emphasis

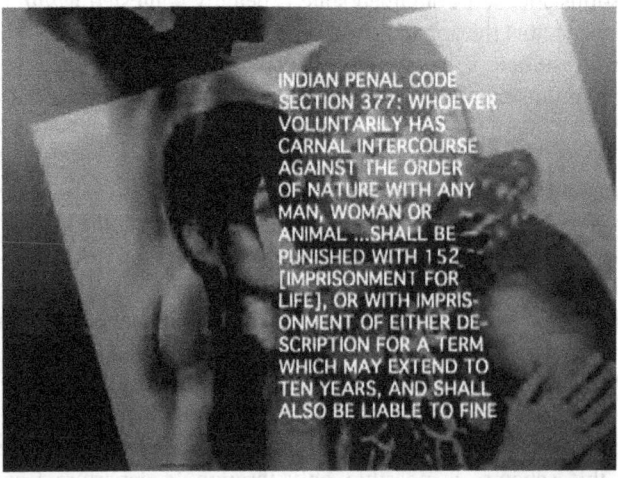

Figure 4. Still from *Milind Soman Made Me Gay* (2007). Directed by Harjant Gill.

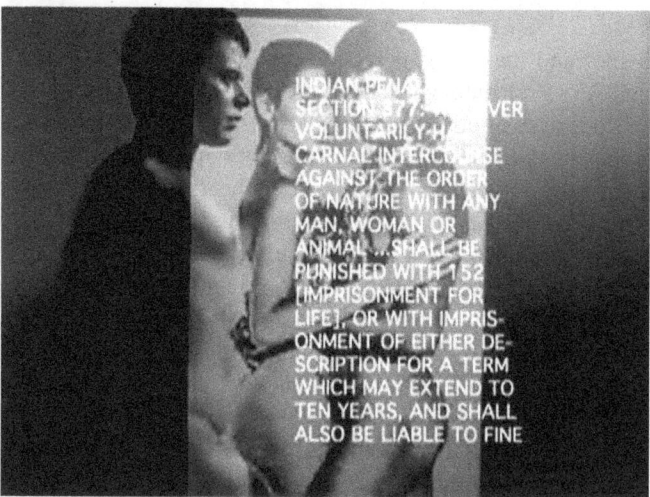

Figure 5. Still from *Milind Soman Made Me Gay* (2007). Directed by Harjant Gill.

on temporal and spatial gaps between the media. Nevertheless, why does Gill – as a gay man of colour in the US – choose to emphasize erotically this particular 'memory'? Why this stitching together of the *naked, ethnic* body, a 'native' model and a colonial law? Why indeed this specific reference to a male body that is 'authentically' Indian? Milind Soman, it is worth remembering, debuted as a performer/actor in Indian pop-star Alisha Chinay's chart-busting mid-nineties number 'Made in India.'[20] Could Gill's use of Soman's body, then, also be seen as a response to a specific *crisis* in the queer-ethnic imaginary? What new structure of artistic narcissism could this intermedial space produce?

On the representation of the Asian body in gay pornography made in the United States, Richard Fung writes:

> The contemporary construction of race and sex ... has endowed black people, both men and women, with a threatening hypersexuality. Asians, on the other hand, are collectively seen as undersexed.... South Asians, people whose backgrounds are in the Indian subcontinent and Sri Lanka, hardly figure at all in North American popular representations, and those few images are ostensibly devoid of sexual connotation.... If we look at commercial gay sexual representations, it appears that the anti-racist movements have had little impact: the images of men and male beauty are still of *white* men and *white* male beauty. These are the standards against which we compare both ourselves and our brothers – Asian, black, native and Latino. Although other people's rejection (or fetishization) of us according to the established racial hierarchies may be experienced as oppressive, we are not necessarily moved to scrutinize our own desire and its relationship to the hegemonic image of the white man. (Fung 116–18)

In other words, Fung is anxious about whiteness maintaining its normativity and producing an almost unattainable 'ideal,' particularly in dominant queer representations. For Fung, an exhibition of the (homo)erotic ethnic body thus becomes a mode self-scrutiny and of recuperation of the narcissism denied. As the epitome of 'Indian masculinity' Soman's body is a 'model' that the ethnic body wants to identify with and claim as its own. Simultaneously, the video itself becomes an occasion for Gill to eroticize his own body.

The body re-members

Throughout the prologue (and the first two sections of the video), Gill places himself between the camera and the screen onto which are projected images from 'home.'[21] As his voiceover speaks of his desire to return to India, Gill turns to grope these images on the screen and creates compositions that evoke both the sensuous and the sensual: he strikes a pose facing the screen, his palms joined above his head, so that the greenish image of lotus buds washes his bare back and momentarily takes on the appearance of fish-scales on his naked torso. The buds make his tattoo emerge as a bas-relief. His shadow exceeds him and finds its place on the screen. However, the image on the screen stops short of penetrating his umbra. Gill stretches his left hand, makes rhythmic wave-like motions, and watches the shadows he creates on the screen. There is yearning in his movements, but there is also an autoerotic element of taking and *seeing* oneself, as the object of pleasure (see Figures 6 and 7).

By shooting the naked erotic self, Gill also invites his viewers to reflect on the intimate relationship between the camera and the object of the camera's gaze. Since Gill, as the video-artist, gazes upon his auto-erotic self, his presence both behind and in front of the camera make his performance doubly auto-erotic and narcissistic. Thus my reference to the scene from the Leonardo essay is not that out of place: this is also Narcissus's turn toward 'his own reflection,' his move toward the 'autoerotic' as an act of self-preservation. Unlike in Freud's Leonardo, however, intermedial queerness, here, is not repressed and does not end here. The affective impact created by this performance is nostalgia for 'home,' but one that is also tied to an eroticized perception of the relation between the self and the other.

Thus, if the prologue establishes diasporic longing in terms of the autoerotic body, the first section of the video begins by mourning the massacre of Sikhs in October 1984 in India. Images of violence and shots of newspaper reports (of both the Indian Partition in 1947 and the Anti-Sikh riots in 1984) play out on the screen and wash Gill's body positioned in front (see Figure 1). As he turns back to look, Gill's voiceover tells us that, being a child in the early eighties, he has 'no memory' of the riots. Yet, he senses the need to 'recollect' the trauma of the massacre of his own community on the surface of his own

Figure 6. Still from *Milind Soman Made Me Gay* (2007). Directed by Harjant Gill.

Figure 7. Still from *Milind Soman Made Me Gay* (2007). Directed by Harjant Gill.

skin. At the same time, he also feels the compulsion to 're-imagine' repeatedly an encounter with someone from the 'enemy' camp, a meeting that perhaps never really took place:

> There are some moments you remember. And some you forget. And there are those you ... we re-imagine over and over again, hoping to make sense of who you are and in relationship to the world around you ... I imagined that I was two years old. The roads are covered with dead bodies. And the area smells of burning flesh. We are looking for a place to hide and a stranger gives us refuge. If it wasn't for him, I would have been killed. He saved my life. He was a Hindu.

Interestingly, this section (called 'Child's Escape') is placed between the autoeroticism of the prologue and the homosexual object-choice scenario of the second section. The third section ('Inescapable Fate') echoes the first, in so far as Gill 'imagines' yet another connection, with yet another other – 'across time' and through an affective and an ethico-sexual component – a white boy killed in a hate crime committed out of homophobia:

> I am seventeen years old. There are some moments you remember. And some you forget. And there are those you re-imagine over and over again, hoping to make sense of who you are and in relationship to the world around you. When I arrived at school that day, everyone told me to be careful. They told me not to be so gay. *I imagined how it might have felt like if I were beaten and tied to a fence, left there to die. I wondered if getting beaten and tied to a fence was something inescapable ... something that every gay person experiences.*

In this section, the close-up of Gill's own (clearly non-white) face is in stark contrast to the spectral whiteness of the image of Shepard projected on the screen. 'Identification' in terms of sexual marginalization ('sameness' in terms of sexuality) is thus also fraught with disidentification, and limited by Gill's consciousness of being an immigrant and possessing a racially marked body: 'I wondered if anyone would have cared, specially because I am not an American, and unlike Matthew, I certainly am not white.' Defined in terms of the antagonisms that characterize relationships in the imaginary,[22] the Sikh's otherness may be perceived differently by the Hindu rioter and the white American who shot Balbir Singh Sodhi. However, what Gill's queer intermediation underscores is the link between the two perceptions: representations of the Sikh's otherness in India (as the 'militant' demanding a separate 'nation' of Khalistan) have a transnational impact on the Sikh community in diaspora – most palpably evinced in the violence against Sikhs in the United States after 9/11. As Gill notes later in the video, 'After September 11, Sikhs became the prime targets of hate crimes as one of the largest and most visible ethnic minorities, mistaken for their appearance, misunderstood for their otherness.' In other words, it is not as if a narcissistic Gill wishes to do away with otherness: his body is, in fact, 'haunted' by 'ghostly returns' of the imaginary Hindu, Shepard and Sodhi; that is to say, bodies that he clearly sees as being marginalized racially and/or sexually. On the ethics of a queer historiography in the writings of Jacques Derrida and Jonathan Goldberg, Carla Freccero notes,

> ... for these writers engaged in an ethical relation to a traumatic past event, the trace that is also a calling, a demand, a messianic wish or hope, takes the troubled form of a ghost – neither altogether present nor quite absent – conjured by the moment of writing. *And it is no coincidence that the figures invoked in these archival memorials are racially and sexually marked, for just as ghostliness designates an ambiguous state of being, both present and not, past and not, so too in these accounts racial mixture and sexual – including sexuality – difference stand in for, even as they mark the material place of, a critique of originary purity, simplicity and unmixedness.*[23]

Freccero also sees these returns as a 'sign of trauma and mourning.' However, the desire to be 'ghosted,' here, is the very *opposite* of the teleological process of Freudian 'mourning.' Gill's video seems to be doing something similar: his 'writing' stems from his ethnic position that uses narcissism to invoke a comparable spectrality, to mourn the sexual, the racial as well as the ethnic other. The idea is not to 'get over' these ghosts, but to visualize alternative trajectories of history on a spectral screen that is also a mirror. Gill's transindividualism is thus inseparable from his auto-eroticism that, paradoxically, at once performs and critiques Freud's description. The artist's intermedial narcissism, one could argue, contiguously aligns different degrees of imaginary otherness, only to get *beyond* the coherence and stability of the imaginary ego. In the final section, I identify two such moments of self-deconstruction in the text.

Performing the limits of representation

The 'ethico-political task of the humanities,' Gayatri Chakravorty Spivak reminds us in her introduction to *Other Asias*, 'has always been the rearrangement of desires,' to look at the pores of texts 'to tease out excluded itineraries' (Spivak 9). This constant rearrangement, I will argue, is not dissimilar from the continual struggle to *queer* queerness, an *askesis* that one undertakes during the 'practice of the self,' without succumbing to the lures of 'teleology' and 'stability.'[24] To 'queer-read' as an *ethical* practice, therefore, would also entail looking for those internal contradictions that 'reveal' the ideological limits of a queer text.[25] In this final section of the paper, I examine the limits of the video that focuses primarily on the confessions of 'South Asian gay men' in diaspora, a category that I see the video itself to be struggling to define. My aim is not to attenuate arguments made so far, but to identify fissures within the representation, to probe further the effects of the performativity of Gill's mimesis.

What, indeed, we might ask as spectators, is the 'South Asianness'[26] conveyed by the men interviewed by Gill in the video? Interestingly, both men who speak of a 'South Asian' identity – Daniel Phoenix Singh and Ayush Gupta – come from India. In addition, it is a *national* identity that both fall back on for self-description: Singh speaks of the connection between being a classical *Indian* dancer and a gay man; Gupta describes the specificity of

Indian culture and the conflict that his *Indian* upbringing creates with his homosexuality. The third interviewee, Salman Shamsi, however, comes from Pakistan, and repeatedly identifies as 'Pakistani.' The shared cultural histories of India and Pakistan are evoked as Shamsi speaks of playing with Indian and Pakistani dolls as a child, and of 'identifying' with the marginalization of courtesans in Bollywood films. Hence all three interviews, perhaps inadvertently, provoke the nagging question: what image of 'South Asia' do these diasporic confessions inscribe, given that, geographically, South Asia comprises six other countries besides India? Any attempt to represent 'South Asianness' – even when 'South Asia' is not a euphemism for membership of elite Indians 'in exile' – will inevitably point towards excluded migrant subjectivities, the dominance of a particular gender and a particular class, and hence of a particular group of ideologies. However, Gill's video, I will argue, also invites critique of identity politics, and *asks* for the interference of his mimesis to be called out. Throughout Gupta's interview, for instance, his white partner Theron is made to 'act' and stand in silence. Following the director's instructions,[27] Theron performs an inexplicable docility that 'inverts' the power relationship that hegemonic whiteness might be presumed to have with an imagined 'South Asianness.' Simultaneously, however, Theron's 'passivity' also performs, even exaggerates the cultural resource and class prerogative that Gupta possesses to be able to *be* in a relationship with a white man. Similarly, cutaways of flower sellers in an Indian bazaar, inserted over Theron's voice, produce a jarring effect and insist on the difference between the speaking subject and the subaltern who is 'seen' but not heard. In other words, this decision to 'perform' agency produces visual slippages and ensures that what the filmmaker and video-artist 'overlooks' or 'ignores' (since the category of 'class' is never brought up explicitly as an issue in the video) cannot be separated from what it seeks to represent – 'the elusive and yet undeniable' South Asian gay identity – what the video suggests it 'knows.' Gill's 'direction' is thus also a 'fiction' that announces its own limits. This sequence then, is 'instructive' precisely because it performs a kind of 'queer pedagogy,' where 'knowledge' and 'ignorance' are not mutually exclusive but rather co-constitutive.[28]

Finally, I want to look at the limits of mimeticism in Gill's video in relation to *sexual difference*, a vexed issue that continues to drive (sexed) wedges in queer theories and practices.[29] I will end by locating another moment of intermedial dissonance, this time a moment of aural slippage that raises the 'spectre' of the queer woman of colour.

Where is the South Asian *lesbian*, the queer feminist of colour, one might ask, in this project that 'redefines' narcissism? Is Echo to be excluded yet again?[30] Does foregrounding the *male* body as an archive not obfuscate multiple narratives of the *female* body as the commonest site for racial, sexual and gendered violence? In ignoring the *female* queer ethnic, does the video not perpetuate the attachment of the male homosexual to phallic masculinity?

While these are legitimate questions, they also provoke the counter-question: what does it even mean to 'represent' a (South Asian) lesbian? As Annamarie Jagose points out:

> ... the familiar figure of the invisible lesbian is animated by a structuring paradox. The persistent rhetorical figuration of lesbianism as unrepresentable, invisible, and impossible brings to representation the very thing that, this very thing this figuration claims, remains outside the visual field. Because lesbian invisibility is precisely, if paradoxically, a strategy of representation – even a strategy of visualization – lesbian visibility cannot be imagined as its redress. (Jagose 2)

Jagose thus draws our attention to *the terms* of representation, to questions of agency, and to larger questions of what 'the lesbian' might gain being coerced into 'seeing' her phantasm in an other's 'mirror' of mimesis. The 'representation' of a lesbian is further complicated by the category of race in the case of queer South Asian women in diaspora, and indeed, non-white queer women in general.

How might we read the 'invisibility' of the lesbian of colour in Gill's video? Immediately after Gupta's interview ends, Gill gives us a 'bridge' sequence shot in a park. The sequence may have been shot in India, but that it is not 'in sequence' (that is, before we see shots of Gill visiting New Delhi) is in keeping with Gill's 'homohistory.'[31] It is a short sequence of two men walking in (or perhaps even cruising) a park on a sunny afternoon. But the song that plays throughout the sequence is 'You Can't Tell the Difference After Dark' by Alberta Hunter. Here, the singer (a woman) regrets being 'brown as a berry,' and the fact that her complexion may have something to do with men staying away from her, choosing blond women instead. At the same time, insisting on her capacity to love and to win over the potential suitor through her love, the singer argues that her complexion should really cease to matter in (as the song's title suggests) the intimate darkness surrounding the lovers.[32]

Could it be a sheer coincidence that this song, disrupting the 'South Asian' gay male 'narrative,' is sung by a queer black woman from the Harlem Renaissance, a black blues singer who was concerned about her sexual 'visibility'; that this is a song that negotiates ambivalence around the racially marked body perhaps desiring whiteness; and that it comes right after the performance of a South Asian gay man's 'agency' in an interracial homosexual relationship? How might we place this song *formally*, in terms of the structure and style of the video?

In his well-known book, *The Voice in Cinema*, Michel Chion defines the 'acousmatic voice' as a diegetic presence that is visually not available to the spectator. The disembodied voice or the *acousmêtre*, Chion suggests, is all-seeing and all-knowing: 'Being in the screen and not, wandering the surface of the screen without entering it, the *acousmêtre* brings tension and disequilibrium. He [sic] invites the spectator to *go see*, and he [sic] can be an invitation to the loss of the self, to desire and fascination' (Chion 24). I want to suggest that the voice of Alberta Hunter gains an acousmatic dimension because her voice blurs lines between the 'diegetic' and the 'extra-diegetic,' and produces the intermedial by colliding with the visual. Performance of 'agency' in Gupta's interview, one could argue, 'fails' precisely when the voice intervenes asking the spectator to 'see' to another 'reality,' even when the visual correlative is not available. This is the effect of the voice that intervenes as 'an instrument of the possibility of a truth not dependent upon intention' (Spivak 24). Without a context for its 'appearance,' the song cannot be directly linked to the female (Hunter's) 'body.' Yet, to the viewer – even if is s/he is not familiar with Hunter's sexual history – the stranger's voice and the lyrics serve as a Brechtian 'interruption.' Like a true *acousmêtre*, who is faceless, incorporeal, unlocatable, and has 'no business being there,' the voice asserts itself, alienates the viewer, and resists visual identification. Like Freccero's spectral sexual-racial outcast, the song retains its power to destabilize *because* the voice remains body-less and visually unrepresented. Thus, Echo makes herself heard, and avoids being 'de-acousmatized' (Chion 27) by not being subordinated to (and hence not buried within) the visibly narcissistic body.

Conclusion

This paper has tried to read the politics of Harjant Gill's *Milind Soman Made Me Gay* as an instance of queer video art in diaspora. It has tried to argue that the narcissism of the video is not just an exercise in self-love, but that it can be read as an intermedia performance that provokes queer-diasporic questions around psychoanalytic formulations of narcissism. On Jean Laplanche's radical reinterpretation of Freud, John Fletcher writes,

> In a formula parodying Haeckel's law of which Freud was so enamoured – 'ontogenesis [the development of the human being] reproduces the stages of phylogenesis [the development of the species]' – Laplanche formulates 'Laplanche's law' in which 'theoreticogenesis,' the development of theory, reproduces ontogenesis, the fate of sexuality and the unconscious in the human being. (Fletcher 3)

In other words, how we 'read' is shaped by both who we are and who we *want* to be. *Reading* the performance of liminality in and the uncertainties of Gill's project, I want to suggest, can also be looked upon a form of 'theoreticogenesis,' an ethical redefinition of the limitations and possibilities of narcissism. In other words, it is within this space of a reflexive reading (no doubt provoked by the video itself) that we might think about bridging what Chow sees as the 'incommensurability between theoretical and non-theoretical writing' (Chow 136). As Althusser notes, 'important theoretical events do not always or exclusively occur in theory: it happens that they also occur in politics' (Althusser 65). In that sense, Gill's camera 'writes' a time that is not just retrospective, but also declarative, in so far as it creates an intermedial zone of exchange, of reception and further production, where 'theory' and 'practice'/'politics' meet, commingle and influence each other's futures.

Notes

1. The two key works in this direction would be David Eng's *Racial Castration* and Anne Anlin Cheng's *The Melancholy of Race*.
2. Leo Bersani's theorization of 'impersonal narcissism' in his recent book *Intimacies* would be an exception. However, narcissism, here, takes its cue from a reading of psychoanalysis that confines itself to sexuality, and is not interested in issues of post-coloniality and race.
3. Jasbir K. Puar discusses this link between terrorism and racialized homosexuality in *Terrorist Assemblages*.
4. To describe the second level, Chow draws upon the work of Frantz Fanon and Homi K. Bhabha. She succinctly summarizes and critiques the poststructuralist turn that Bhabha's notions of 'mimicry' and the 'split' subject gives to Fanon's theories of the colonized psyche. Chow rightly concludes that this post-structuralist, psychoanalytic model cannot concretely identify *who* benefits from these openings, fissures and ambivalences. In other words, what seems to be missing from Bhabha's theory is the specific *context* of the diasporic and/or postcolonial subject's experience. For her analysis of both the first and second levels of mimeticism, see Chow 103–27.
5. I use the term 'ethnic' being fully aware of the tension *within* the prevalent notion of 'ethnicity,' its simultaneous claims for the 'universal' and the 'particular.' What I am emphasizing, here, is the more powerful force of ghettoization at work in the concept. Chow herself comments on the contradiction between the shift in the modern use of the concept of ethnicity (from minoritizing exclusion to universalizing inclusion) and the actual violence that marks the term's political deployment. See Chow 24–30.
6. See in particular, Chow's reading of the last piece in Hongo's book – John Yau's 'A Little Memento from the Boys.' See Chow 147–52.
7. 'Queerness,' here, is a shorthand for the politics of non-heteronormative. 'Queer of colour' and 'queer-diasporic' are terms I use to emphasize the interarticulation of 'race' and 'homosexuality,' and the dominant whiteness of canonical 'queer theory.'
8. Abandoning J. L. Austin's favourite example 'I do' – a performative in the 'first person singular present indicative active' and tied to the context of a heterosexual state-sanctioned Christian marriage – Sedgwick chooses the performative 'Shame on you!' to explore the (queer) performativity of a 'debased' emotion like 'shame' through her analysis of the Prefaces of Henry James. It is important to note the difference in the strategies used by Butler and Sedgwick to arrive at performativity. Sedgwick attempts to tease out that moment of *bouleversement* by

questioning Austin's definition of the performative utterance and turning to a blatantly more injurious and humiliating instance. Butler, however, sees *compulsive repetition* as itself being destabilizing and failing to secure the identity of the speaking 'I.' See Sedgwick 1–16; Butler *Bodies that Matter*.

9. Etienne Balibar uses the term 'fictive ethnicity' for that formation that is imposed on a group of people by the nation-state. Ethnicity is 'fictive' in the sense that the imposition or construction is sutured over by representations of linguistic, racial and/or religious 'unity.' See Balibar 96.

10. On the notion of resistance through iteration, Butler writes: 'performance as a bounded 'act' is distinguished from performativity in so far as the latter consists in a reiteration of norms which precede, constrain, and exceed the performer and in that sense cannot be taken as the fabrication of the performer's 'will' or 'choice'; further, what is 'performed' works to conceal, if not disavow, what remains opaque, unconscious, unperformable. The reduction of performativity to performance would be a mistake.' See Butler 234.

11. For a discussion of this defining aspect of intermedia, see Spielmann 133.

12. I am borrowing the phrases that Chow uses specifically for Hongo's collection, because the larger context of her analysis is the immigrant artist's turn toward herself. See Chow 142–52.

13. I am, here, alluding to Rosalind Krauss's famous dictum: 'The medium of video is narcissism.' Krauss reaches her conclusion through her analysis of self-reflection and encapsulation in contemporary video art. She makes a distinction between narcissistic 'reflection' in video and the 'reflexive' turn in contemporary painting, sculpture and film. Gill's narcissism, I will argue, disrupts this reflection/reflexivity binary. See Krauss 50–64.

14. Chow 145.

15. Around 4000 Sikhs died in the anti-Sikh riots that broke out in India after her Sikh bodyguard assassinated Indian Prime Minister Indira Gandhi. It has now been proved that members of the ruling Congress party were involved in organizing the riots.

    Model and Bollywood actor Milind Soman and his co-star Madhu Sapre faced obscenity charges (under Section 292 of the Indian Penal Code) for appearing nude in an advertisement for a brand of sports shoes in the mid-nineties. The same law was frequently used with IPC 377 (the law that, until recently, criminalized 'unnatural' sexual acts including anal sex) to harass and arrest homosexuals, sex-workers and outreach workers in India.

    Defendants in the Matthew Shepard case used 'homosexual panic' to justify the murder of Shepard in Wyoming in October 1998. His assailants, Russell Arthur Henderson and Aaron James McKinney, finally pleaded guilty. Shepard's murder brought to the fore inconsistencies in 'hate crime' legislation at the state and federal levels in the United States.

    Balbir Singh Sodhi, a Sikh gas station owner, was murdered by Frank Roque in Mesa, Arizona on 15 September 2001. Roque, as Gill's video reminds us, shouted, 'I stand for America all the way' as he shot Sodhi, apparently mistaking him for a 'Middle Eastern' because of his turban. Legal scholar Muneer Ahmed has shown how media representations in the US sought to rationalize Sodhi's murder in the context of 'nationalism': 'To borrow from criminal law, the hate crime killings before September 11 were viewed as crimes of moral depravity, while the hate killings since September 11 have been understood as crimes of passion' (108). In other words, Sodhi's murder did not provoke the same 'hate crime' outrage that Shepard's murder had. See Ahmed 101–15.

16. The (m)other need not be the biological mother, but any one who takes on the role of the caregiver and nurturer. See Green 73.

17. Fanon's turn to the 'mirror stage' is worth remembering: For Fanon, writing in the context of racism in the colonial Antilles, the identity of the ego is not grounded in specularity alone, but inextricably tied to a conscious and acute awareness of the corporeal black body marked by visible phenotypic difference. See Fanon 161.

18. Reading *Totem and Taboo* alongside 'On Narcissism,' David Eng convincingly argues that there is a marked affinity between Freud's account of homosexual narcissism and the 'stalled mental life of savages.' That is to say, in Eng's argument, Freud's anxiety around racial difference manifests itself as homosexuality that the socialized subject must overcome. See Eng 9–12.

19. Freud, here, is specifically talking about the male homosexual. See Freud 'On Narcissism' 80. I must hasten to add that the essay, even as it pathologizes homosexuality, also hints at the inevitably narcissistic nature of the human psyche. 'Secondary narcissism,' in Freud's view, is the desperate attempt of every ego to recapture its primary narcissism.

20. In this video, Soman plays a suitor to an 'oriental' princess (played by Chinay herself): clad in just a dhoti, Soman comes out of a box marked 'Made in India,' and impresses the princess with his looks and his chiselled 'Indian' physique.
21. The 'South Asian' body is also highlighted when Gill interviews dancer Daniel Phoenix Singh in the video. As Singh speaks, the 'cutaways' underscore his svelte, muscular body as we see him perform in front of the camera. Singh's presence in the video could also be compared to that of a character like 'Beauty' in Isaac Julien's *Looking for Langston*. In other words, the exhibitionistic body in Gill's video could also be seen to aim to construct, 'from scratch,' an ethnic model of what constitutes the 'homo-erotic' and the 'homosexual.' The body, here, is not crushed by its refusal to emulate whiteness. Neither does it fear existing as a 'bad' copy.
22. By 'imaginary' relationships, Lacan means relationships that are based on the image of the self. The 'other,' seen as a rival, is thus perceived to be either 'similar' to or 'different' from the self.
23. See Frecerro 85.
24. In 'Friendship as a Way of Life,' Foucault writes, 'Homosexuality is not a form of desire but something desirable. Therefore, we have to work at becoming homosexuals and not be obstinate in recognizing that we are.' See Foucault 136. Moreover, in 'The Hermeneutic of the Subject,' Foucault writes that the care of the self 'has a function of struggle. The practice of the self is conceived of as permanent battle. It is not simply a matter of shaping a man of valour for the future.' See Foucault 97.
25. On mimesis as a 'reflection' of reality, Pierre Macherey writes: 'The mirror is expressive in what it does not reflect as much as in what it does reflect. The absence of certain reflections, expressions – these are the true object of criticism.' See Macherey 143.
26. Here is the description of the video on the website of Gill's production company: '*Milind Soman Made Me Gay* ... employs a unique mix of visual elements along with voice over narration to juxtapose memories of the filmmaker's past against stories of three gay South Asian men living in the diaspora.' See http://www.tilotamaproductions.com/FILMS.html
27. In an (yet unpublished) article and in response to a review of the video, Gill writes:

> 'To deny Theron a voice within the context of this documentary was also an intentional decision that I made as a director. Even though there is an undeniable and tense sense of racial hierarchy within the mainstream depictions of gay and lesbian life in the US, I didn't want the viewers to conclude that gay South Asian men lack agency.' (Gill 'How Milind Soman Made Me Gay' 6).

28. Deborah P. Britzman points out that to 'queer-read' would entail realising that 'the relationship between knowledge and ignorance is neither opposite nor binary.' Knowledge and ignorance, Britzman argues, mutually implicate each other, structuring and enforcing particular forms of knowledge and particular forms of ignorance. See Britzman 154.
29. Tim Dean, for instance, critiques the tendency of feminist psychoanalysis to privilege sexual difference. Yet, for his own theory of sameness, he 'questions the plausibility of discussing men's and women's homosexualities as if they could be comprehended within the terms of a single conceptual model.' See Dean 121.
30. I am, here, referring to Spivak's deconstructive reading of the myth of Narcissus in her seminal essay 'Echo.' While Spivak ultimately reads Echo (the nymph that Narcissus spurned) as the subaltern woman in the global 'south,' I borrow her initial formulation of Ovid's Echo (who is completely missing from psychoanalytic appropriations of the myth of Narcissus) as the potential for deconstruction and *différance*. See Spivak 17–43.
31. Jonathan Goldberg and Madhavi Menon define 'homohistory' as being opposed to the history of the 'homos,' and invested in possibilities of anachronism and a movement beyond sexual identity. See Goldberg and Menon 1609.
32. I was unable to cite the lyrics of the song because of copyright issues. However, my paper summarizes the stanza that Gill includes in the video. The lyrics of Hunter's song are available at http://www.justsomelyrics.com/1660451/Alberta-Hunter-You-Can%27t-Tell-The-Difference-After-Dark-Lyrics. Lilian Faderman writes that Hunter married in 1919, so that people she knew stopped seeing her as a 'bulldiker.' Pretending to be 'bisexual,' Faderman writes, was apparently an easier solution in the sophisticated circuits of Harlem. See Faderman 75.

Notes on contributor

Ani Maitra is a graduate student in the Department of Modern Culture and Media at Brown University, with interests in queer diasporic film, video and literature, working at the intersection of queer theory, psychoanalysis, and critical race theory. His publications include 'The Flight of the Eunuch: Mapping Homotextualities in South Asian Diaspora Literature' in the anthology *Anxieties, Influences and After: Critical Responses to Postcolonialism and Neocolonialism* (New Delhi: Worldview Publications, 2008); and 'Why Isn't Michelle Lopez on *Judge Judy?* Citizenship and Televisuality in Hima B.'s *And I Do Survive*,' forthcoming in *Camera Obscura* 74, Volume 25, Number 2. Before coming to Brown, Ani worked as a TV journalist in New Delhi.

References

Ahmed, Muneer. "Homeland Insecurities: Racial Violence the Day After September 11." *Social Text* 20.3 (2002): 101–15. Print.

Althusser, Louis. "On Theoretical Work." *Philosophy and the Spontaneous Philosophy of Scientists.* London: Verso, 1997. 65. Print.

Balibar, Etienne. "The Nation Form: History and Ideology." *Race, Nation, Class: Ambiguous Identities.* Trans. Chris Turner. Ed. Etienne Balibar and Emmanuel Wallerstein. London and New York: Verso, 1991. 86–106. Print.

Bersani, Leo, and Adam Phillips. *Intimacies.* Chicago: U of Chicago P, 2008. Print.

Breder, Hans. "Enacting the Liminal." *Intermedia: Enacting the Liminal.* Ed. Hans Breder and Klauss-Peter Busse. Dortmund: Schriften zur Kunst, 2005. 203–15. Print.

Britzman, Deborah. "Is There a Queer Pedagogy? Or, Stop Reading Straight." *Educational Theory* 45.2 (1995): 154. Print.

Butler, Judith. *Bodies that Matter: On the Discursive Limits of "Sex".* New York: Routledge, 1993. Print.

Cheng, Anne Anlin. *The Melancholy of Race: Psychoanalysis, Assimilation and Hidden Grief.* New York: Oxford UP, 2001. Print.

Chion, Michel. *The Voice in Cinema.* Trans. Claudia Gorbman. New York: Columbia UP, 1999. Print.

Chow, Rey. *The Protestant Ethnic and the Spirit of Capitalism.* New York: Columbia UP, 2002. Print.

Cohen, Josh. "'I-no-I': Narcissism Beyond the One and the Other." *Narcissism: A Critical Reader.* Ed. Anastasios Gaitanidies and Plona Curk. London: Karnac Books, 2007. 31–46. Print.

Dean, Tim. "Homosexuality and the Problem of Otherness." *Homosexuality and Psychoanalysis.* Ed. Tim Dean and Christopher Lane. Chicago and London: U of Chicago P, 2001. 120–46. Print.

Eng, David L. *Racial Castration: Managing Masculinity in Asian America.* Durham: Duke UP, 2001. Print.

Faderman, Lilian. *Odd Girls and Twilight Lovers: A History of Lesbian Life in Twentieth Century America.* New York: Columbia UP, 1991. Print.

Fanon, Frantz. *Black Skine White Masks.* Trans. Charles Lam Markmann. New York: Grove Press, 1967. Print.

Fletcher, John. "Introduction: Psychoanalysis and the Question of the Other." *Essays on Otherness.* Ed. John Fletcher. Florence, KY: Routledge, 1993. 1–52. Print.

Foucault, Michel. *Ethics: Subjectivity and Agency. Vol 1: Essential Works of Foucault, 1954–1997.* Ed. Paul Rainbow. New York: The New Press, 1997. Print.

Frecerro, Carla. *Queer/Early/Modern.* Durham: Duke UP, 2005. Print.

Freud, Sigmund. "Leonardo Da Vinci and a Memory of His Childhood." 1910. *The Standard Edition of the Complete Psychological Works of Sigmund Freud.* Trans. and ed. J. Strachey. Vol. 2. London: Hogarth Press, 1961. 59–138. Print.

Freud, Sigmund. "On Narcissism: An Introduction." 1963. *General Psychological Theory: Papers on Metapsychology.* New York: Simon & Schuster, 1993. 56–82. Print.

Fung, Richard. "Looking for My Penis: The Eroticized Asian in Gay Video Porn." *How Do I Look? Queer Film and Video.* Ed. Bad-Object Choices. Seattle: Bay Press, 1991. 116–8. Print.

Gill, Harjant. "How Milind Soman Made Me Gay: Interrogating Belonging and Citizenship." *The Anthropologist* (2010): forthcoming. Print.

Gill, Harjant, dir. *Milind Soman Made Me Gay.* Tilotama Productions, 2007. DVD.

Goldberg, Jonathan, and Mahavi Menon. "Queering History." *PMLA* 120.5 (October 2005): 1608–17. Print.

Green, André. *Life Narcissism Death Narcissism*. Trans. A. Weller. London: Free Association Books, 2001. Print.

Hongo, G., ed. *Under Western Eyes: Personal Essays from Asian America*. New York: Anchor/Doubleday, 1995. Print.

Jagose, Annamarie. *Inconsequence: Lesbian Representation and the Logic of Sexual Sequence*. Ithaca and London: Cornell UP, 2002. Print.

Klemm, David E. "Intermedial Being." *Intermedia: Enacting the Liminal*. Ed. Hans Breder and Klauss-Peter Busse. Dortmund: Schriften Zur Kunst, 2005. 67–78. Print.

Krauss, Rosalind. "Video: The Aesthetics of Narcissism." *October* 1 (1976): 50–64. Print.

Lacan, Jacques. *Écrits: A Selection*. 1977. Trans. Alan Sheridan. London and New York: Routledge, 2007. Print.

Laplanche, Jean. *Essays on Otherness*. Florence, KY: Routledge, 1993. Print.

Laplanche, Jean. *Life and Death in Psychoanalysis*. 1976. Trans. J. Mehlman. Baltimore: Johns Hopkins UP, 1985.

LeCarré, John. "A War We Cannot Win." *The Nation* 19 Nov. 2001: 15–17. Print.

Macherey, Pierre. *A Theory of Literary Production*. 1978. Trans. Geoffrey Wall. London and New York: Routledge, 2005. Print.

Muñoz, José Esteban. *Cruising Utopia: The Then and There of Queer Futurity*. New York and London: New York UP, 2009.

Puar, Jasbir K. *Terrorist Assemblages: Homonationalism in Queer Times*. Durham: Duke UP, 2007. Print.

Sedgwick, Eve Kosofsky. "Queer Performativity: Henry James's *The Art of the Novel*." *The Lesbian and Gay Quarterly* 1 (1993): 1–16. Print.

Spielmann, Yvonne. "History and Theory of Intermedia in Visual Culture." *Intermedia: Enacting the Liminal*. Ed. Hans Breder and Klause-Peter Busse. Dortmund: Schriften Zur Kunst, 2005. 131–8. Print.

Spivak, Gayatri Chakravorty. "Echo." *New Literary History* 24.1 (1993): 17–43. Print.

Spivak, Gayatri Chakravorty. *Other Asias*. Oxford: Blackwell, 2008. Print.

Zee TV: Diasporic non-terrestrial television in Europe[1]

Rajinder Dudrah

> We are your voice, the voice of the Asian community. (Subash Chandra, Founder and Chief Executive, Zee TV)

Diasporic mediascapes

As a way of thinking about national identities in a period of unprecedented transnational movement, the metaphor of the 'diaspora' has gained widespread currency in the humanities and social sciences (Appadurai; Robertson; Tololyan; Anthias). The term points towards a form of identity formation that is neither pure nor fixed, and that holds in play the experiences of migrant people and successive settled generations – their relationships with a country of origin and countries of settlement, and their diasporic consciousness or imagination that shifts between these two coordinates.

Recent work has recognised the importance of media in the formation of diasporic communities and identities. Television, and other forms of popular culture, can serve an 'epistephilic' desire for information such as current affairs and information about 'selfhood' (Naficy, 106–8).[2] They can offer diasporic viewers representations of who they are, and who their communities might be. They can supply the basis from which scripts can be formed of actual and imagined lives, of selves and others in near and faraway places (Appadurai; Appadurai 'Modernity').

Zee TV-Europe is a non-terrestrial television channel[3] that caters for diasporic South Asian viewers – with origins in India, Bangladesh and Pakistan – across Western Europe. As the comments of its chief executive above make clear, Zee TV-Europe represents itself precisely in terms of offering services of community- and identity-formation. This chapter examines the forms of identity that are being offered to this diasporic community, and the degree to which Zee-TV Europe succeeds in making such an identity available in a largely white European mediascape.

Representing minorities within European identity

Black representation in European media is constrained in particular ways. It is important to note, in relation to questions of identity formation, that the term 'Black' in this context refers to an anti-racist category, in common use in western Europe, that represents the common experiences of colonialism and contemporary racism in the cultural and social realms for African, Caribbean, and South Asian communities in Britain and throughout Western Europe more generally – a political colour of resistance.[4] The terms 'black' and 'Asian/South Asian' are used to connote specificities in terms of ethnic origin, region and cultural practices and are illustrated throughout the chapter where necessary.

Recent academic studies have illustrated the ambiguous position, at best, which Black people have been assigned in dominant versions of European identity constructed amidst the 'opening up' of the continent in 1992 and the creation of the European Single Market (Back and Nayak). What has become increasingly apparent is that Europe is unrestricted for select social groups only – most often white professional elites. The most marginalized of minority groups are those whose nationality is closely associated with skin colour: Algerians in France, Turks in Germany, Africans, Caribbeans and South Asians in Britain. As Les Back and Anoop Nayak note:

> Simply put, the prevailing common sense is that Europeans are white, while non-Europeans are Black. The immediate danger here is that "Black" and "European" are being reproduced as mutually exclusive categories. The "new Europe" is being defined through a "pan-European whiteness" which excludes Black people. This move signals a new era in the development of racism in Europe. What is emerging is a shift from national forms of ethnocentric racism to a Eurocentric racism which is being established and institutionalized in all the EC member states. (Back and Nayak 4)

Recent studies have shown that contemporary examples of exclusion and discrimination experienced by Black people in urban European cities are rife, and the further threat of Eurocentric racism is one not to be taken lightly (Nayak; Nayak 'Pale Warriors'; Modood and Werbner; Dudrah, 'Birmingham, UK').[5]

The mainstream media of the EC member states have also been shown to disseminate and construct problematic images of Black minorities, thereby fuelling 'Euro-whiteness' (see for instance Ross on the representation of Black people in the mainstream media in Britain). Television programmes which are aimed specifically at non-white groups tend to be constructed explicitly as 'minority' programming[6] (see Cohen and Gardner; Gilroy; Ross (Chapter 5); Cottle; and Malik).[7] In Britain during the early to mid-2000s, a number of such 'minority' programmes were shown: in magazine formats, documentary series, and as film and drama imports from South Asia which were shown intermittently as part of a season or series of programmes throughout the year. The composition of regular minority television in Britain throughout this period included BBC2's *Black Britain*, *Network East*, and *East*, and Central Television's *Eastern Mix*. On the whole, these programmes were presented as being by and for 'minorities' – 'others' and not part of the mainstream of British broadcasting scheduling and its concomitant identities.

Other programmes in the last decade or more, such as the BBC's comedy sketch show *Goodness Gracious Me* (2000), the BBC's comedy chat show format of *The Kumars at No. 42* (2001), and Channel 4's television series of Zadie Smith's novel *White Teeth* (2002) have been interesting achievements in British television that have articulated a more complex sense of British cultural identity through television address. However, such programmes have been possible as a result of the ongoing struggles by Black media professionals for access to the means of production for more elaborate Black representation (cf. Cottle; Malik (Chapter 1)). Whilst these latter programmes are far and few between, on the whole there still appears to be little space available in the British broadcasting schedule for programmes which offer Black – *British* identities – hybrid or diasporic ways of thinking about identity that can encompass both the British culture in which these audiences are living, and the original homelands to which they wish to retain a sense of connectedness. It is in such a context that Zee TV Europe appears.

Yeh Zee TV Kya Hai? – What is Zee TV?

Zee TV is the most successful and popular Hindi and South Asian languages subscription television channel across South Asia, Europe, Africa and North America (Risaluddin; Wanvari 17) as well as parts of the Middle East, and East Asia. It was originally broadcast on the South Beam of the Asiasat-1 satellite, received either by satellite dish, by cable, or by digital network. By the mid-nineties it was also estimated that Zee TV reached 15 out of 40 million homes in India alone (Singh 9) making it the main rival of India's state owned Doordarshan channels (Banerjee; Thussu). In addition, it is popular among non-resident Indians, Pakistanis and Bangladeshis around the world.

Zee TV-Europe took over from the former TV Asia channel in March 1995. TV Asia was launched in July 1992 by a number of non-resident Indian and Pakistani investors as part of a business venture of the Dolphin Media Group, itself owned by South Asian businessmen (Hebbar). TV Asia was western Europe's first subscription satellite television channel specifically targeting European communities of Indian, Pakistani, and Bangladeshi origin (TV Asia). In 1994, TV Asia was experiencing significant financial problems and boardroom struggles, thus allowing Zee TV to move in and take over (Hebbar; Wanvari 17).

Until January 2000, Zee TV was an independent member of the STAR TV (Satellite Television Asia Region) group, which is owned by Rupert Murdoch's News Corporation Ltd (News Corporation). After private talks between Subhash Chandra (Zee TV's chief executive) and Rupert Murdoch, Chandra acquired News Corporation's 50 per cent stake in the broadcasting company Asia Today Ltd, software company Programme Asia Trading Co., and distribution company SitiCable Network for an estimated $300 million. Zee TV uses the services provided by these companies to broadcast across the entire Asia region. This deal made ATL, SitiCable, and PATCO wholly owned subsidiaries of Zee International, allowing Chandra to control a fully integrated media company from programming and broadcasting to global distribution (Chhaya).[8] Zee TV-Europe has a steady and growing number of subscriptions. Currently, it is estimated that there are about 500,000 South Asian households in Britain. Zee TV-Europe has around 150,000 subscribers, accounting for approximately 30% of British South Asian households (Balakrishnan 8).

Zee TV's schedule in Europe combines South Asian and Western programme formats. Its programming includes popular South Asian films from Bangladesh, Pakistan, Sri Lanka and other parts of India, in addition to its main feature films from Bollywood.[9] These, together with a range of other news, current affairs and business programmes, religious, comedy, film review, and health shows, and drama serials from India and Pakistan, as well as South Asian sports, form the basis of the Zee TV schedule. The schedule is uniform right across Europe – and, therefore, can be seen to offer possibilities of an audio-visual pan-South Asian European identity.[10]

Zee TV-Europe and the construction of a pan-South Asian European identity?

In a direct address to Zee TV-Europe's audiences as part of the channel's second anniversary celebration on 3 March 1997, Zee TV's founder and Chief Executive Subhash Chandra sat comfortably on a sofa in a studio and spoke about the growth of Zee TV across the globe and his vision for the channel in Europe. The conversion of studio space into that resembling a domestic setting created a moment of familiarity interpolating Zee viewers as a larger family unit across Europe. During his 15-minute speech, Chandra assured viewers that Zee TV would help South Asians to 'participate fully in their respective countries' as the channel should be used as a 'tool to express your feelings', going on to say that 'we [Zee TV] are your voice, the voice of the Asian community'. Chandra announced his ambitious global vision for the channel wherein it would be a way of 'networking' the 1.5 billion South Asians with each other around the world, starting by 'networking' South Asians in Europe, and networking South Asian Europeans with South Asians in the subcontinent through news and information, entertainment, and community events.

The programming styles presented on TV continue this promise. Signatures such as: 'It keeps you connected'; 'Zee TV *Aap Ka Apna*' (Zee TV is your very own); 'Zee TV for me, for you, for us'; 'Zee TV Bringing You Closer'; and so forth, are presented at the beginning and end of programmes. In addition, direct welcoming gestures are deployed from each of the main South Asian faiths of Hinduism (*Namaste*), Islam (*Asailaam Wale Ghum*), and Sikhism (*Sat Sri Akal*), alongside greetings in English. These gestures play an important role in offering an identity to a diasporic community.

Most importantly, for this chapter the schedule of Zee TV includes several programmes, which claim to represent the South-Asian community in Europe to itself. *Your Zindagi* (Your Life) and *Euro Zindagi* (Euro Life) are magazine-style programmes that feature members of this community. *Your Zindagi* is filmed in the UK and *Euro Zindagi* is filmed across Western Europe during the summer months from June – August at the time of public gatherings such as Asian *melas* (carnivals) and religious festivals. These programmes are shown twice weekly during the summer months and depict South Asians in their everyday home, work and leisure settings throughout Western Europe, partaking in discussions about South Asian and European life, and re-enacting aspects of South Asian popular culture. Taken together with other Zee programmes such as *Out and About*, a UK community events diary programme, and *Public Demand*, an imported popular Bollywood discussion programme from the streets of India, the 'out in the community' programmes attempt to directly address Zee TV viewers.

Your Zindagi and *Euro Zindagi* are the focus of this chapter. By combining textual analysis with interviews with viewers of these programmes, I want to examine the kind of South-Asian-European identity they construct, and examine how some viewers respond to that address. Twenty-three extended interviews were conducted with 14 to 26-year-old South Asians in Birmingham.[11]

Successful community address

Your Zindagi and *Euro Zindagi* follow a similar format. Both tend to begin with introduction to the city or place they are visiting in terms of its importance for South Asians living there. They present interviews with prominent Asian public figures who have been active in the community. They often cover public events in the areas; and include interviews with members of the public on current affairs issues pertaining to the subcontinent and in their places of residence in Europe. There is also a 'Star Spot', which invites members of the public to sing their favourite Bollywood songs or to recite film dialogues. In 1998, *Your Zindagi* visited the summer *melas* at Leicester, Bradford, Manchester, Croydon, Cardiff, and Glasgow.

The viewers of Zee TV to whom I spoke made clear that they are aware of the need to represent a South-Asian-European community, and felt that *Your Zindagi* and *Euro Zindagi* contributed to that process.

> Mozibur: Programmes like *Your Zindagi* and *Euro Zindagi* represent what people collectively like. There's bits of chit chat, discussion, clips from the latest movies, getting people involved to sing and dance so they actually involve people ... It's nice seeing everyday Asian people on the street just chatting about trivial and important things. Whether it's film entertainment or news it's giving them a voice and we see ourselves in those snippets of comments. It's good to see ourselves in that way through the sights and sounds.

Indeed, we can see this process of community formation at work by looking at the way in which viewers become involved in the programmes themselves. A few weeks in advance of each episode, *Your Zindagi* and *Euro Zindagi* advertise which public gatherings they will attend and encourage viewers 'to come along and meet your favourite presenters and take part'. The programmes become part of the community event, rather than simply representing it. During August 1998, the *Euro Zindagi* production team went to an outdoor *mela* organized by the Indo-German Association in Düsseldorf, Germany. The presenters interviewed attendees, asking questions including: 'how did you come to hear about the *mela*?'; 'what is it like to live in Düsseldorf?'; 'do you like it here?'; 'how often do you think of "home" back in South Asia?'; 'is Europe your home?'; and 'what do you think of Zee TV?' Answers included:

> We are here because we saw the advert on Zee TV. We travelled 200 kilometres just to be here ... More of these gatherings should happen.(Middle-aged male)

> Zee has a done a good job. It's uniting our people and our children are learning a bit about our culture. (Early thirties female)

> I have been watching Zee TV for three years now and in those three years, I can't recall switching over to a German channel. Watching Zee TV feels like I'm sitting in India. (Elderly male)

Zee TV has drawn these people together and formed the community that can now be represented – a pan-European South Asian diasporic identity.

Hybrid diasporic identities

It is important to note that the identity being addressed by these Zee TV programmes cannot be simply mapped onto any Asian country; nor on to any European country. Rather, it is a complex mixture of both originary countries, and new homelands. Both 'South-Asian' and 'European' are constantly evolving and heterogeneous identities. Yet, Zee TV seems to succeed in addressing a diasporic community that brings these terms together.

Mozibur: It was good to see Asians in Bradford on *Your Zindagi*. I had visited Bradford just a while back to see my cousins and it was good to see bits of the city again on the telly. I was thinking of the places I had visited and seeing the programme brought some memories back. The accents as well came back and seeing and hearing Asians speak differently reminded me of me and my cousins.

RD: Reminded you in what ways?

Mozibur: Like, the differences in accents and the way we speak our English and Asian languages differently.

Further comments from the Düsseldorf *mela* make similar points about overlapping, and yet shared, identities:

> Düsseldorf, it's good for work and education opportunities for the children, but sometimes I miss Pakistan and my family there. (Middle-aged female)

> It's important to be part of Europe. Like I'm German and European but I won't forget my cultural heritage or mother tongue. (Late-teens male)

Notions of belonging in Europe and affiliations with the country of origin are common points of reference in the *Euro Zindagi* programme. Total assimilation into a predominantly white European culture is impossible and undesirable. Countries of origin provide signs and cues for identification, memory, oral and personal histories, language, politics and so forth. Moreover, these signs and cues are translated and adapted according to the context of people's everyday lives in Europe as amalgamated cultures with possibilities for new and emerging identities: as for example in seeing and hearing South Asian languages spoken with varied European accents. The referents of belonging in and affiliations with Europe and South Asia are what unite *Euro Zindagi's* audience across the continent as an identifiable and discursive social collective in general terms, but this is usually done within the specificities of being geographically located in different towns and cities:

RD: What did you think about seeing different Asians in Europe?

Rita: It was interesting to see so many Asians in different parts of Europe I was surprised how many there were actually. At the *melas* it was nice to see the *jalebis* and *luddoos* (South Asian sweets) and to see people dancing bhangra. Even though their accents were different, I could relate with them, as we all seem to be speaking more or less the same languages and were watching the same films. It was nice to see and learn that Bollywood isn't just popular in Britain.

RD: What did you think of the different European accents?

Rita: Yeah that was nice. Just like I speak fluent English they were also speaking French or German or whatever. They were very much settled over there just like us here.

Another respondent, Bally, pointed out that mainstream media simply did not allow for the possibility of such pan-European South-Asian identities:

RD: What did you think about seeing different Asians in Europe?

Bally: You know I didn't realise that so many Asians were living abroad in Europe. Like I didn't know so many were living and settled in Holland, there were quite a few. I just couldn't imagine it because you're usually told Asians and other people are immigrants just wanting to come to Britain and live off the government.

RD: Who tells you this?

Bally: Well reports in the main news, and the newspapers.

The insistent representation of non-white Europeans as forever 'immigrants' in the countries in which they settle is challenged by images on Zee TV of European citizens who, while not denying their cultural heritage, are fully settled Europeans (see Back and Nayak; Nayak; Modood and Werbner):

RD: So do you think Zee TV helps counteract that impression of Asians as "pakis"?

Bally: Oh yeah, and it's not just Indians or Pakistanis. I remember seeing on that programme (*Euro Zindagi* in Holland) people also from Afghanistan and Sri Lanka as well. Programmes on Zee are good because they can help you appreciate what you are on your own terms ... The second and third generation have come to learn that by becoming one hundred per cent British doesn't take them very far because racism does still exist. Like, for example, they can't change their colour, they might become or think they are one hundred per cent British but they can't change their colour and they'll be viewed as Asians or whatever first. So yeah, Zee TV is important in that way. It's another channel for me now, important as BBC1 and BBC2.

Programmes such as *Your Zindagi* and *Euro Zindagi* on Zee TV offer European South Asian viewers the possibility of imagining alternative scripts that legitimate their lives as bona fide Europeans with dual and multiple sensibilities.

The analysis of the *Your Zindagi* and *Euro Zindagi* programmes also suggests that the signs and codes of what it means to be, and how one is able to imagine oneself as, culturally European can be eclectic and diverse granted the appropriate means of representation. Furthermore, whereas a longstanding and ongoing debate exists at the levels of mainstream popular culture, politics and economics in terms of Britain's love–hate relationship with the European continent (not least in terms of whether Britain should join the single European currency cf. Sardou), my respondents appear to see themselves comfortably as British *and* European *and* Asian through the varied representations depicted through the lens of the Zee TV-Europe channel.

Conclusion and postscript

Of course, the South-Asian-European identities offered on Zee TV are not endlessly inclusive. As with all identities, they rely on exclusion as much as inclusion. Firstly, and obviously, Zee TV-Europe is a pay-TV channel, so its audiences must have a certain degree of economic power to become part of its posited South-Asian diasporic community in Europe (see Murdock; Skovmand and Schroder; Humphreys; Morley and Robins; Sinclair *et al*. 1–5; King; Thussu 'Infotainment'). Beyond this, at least one of my respondents felt that the programming on the channel tailored its address specifically to middle-class Asian audiences:

Mozibur: There's a recognizable format which is built for a certain audience in mind which Zee is trying to capture, and in Britain you could call them the "up and coming Asians", and in India the context would be the middle classes. That's where I find the friction and it comes across strongly in the lifestyle programmes such as *The Low Calorie Show*. A middle class mindset of issues is being addressed. That programme *Kurekshetra* (imported adult studio discussion show from India), the etiquette of how people conduct themselves is interesting. You know it's not trashy television but then it doesn't open up a space for those who don't fit in. Some of the adverts as well have happy middle class Asian families and that's fine but it's not representative of all the people who watch Zee.

Mozibur identifies what he terms as 'middle class mindset' in operation through some of Zee TV-Europe's programmes. He cites a discussion show from India as being invested heavily with 'polite' codes of conduct and moralistic agendas that can be off-putting if you do not subscribe to them or do not possess similar cultural competencies. Middle- to high-income earning Asians are also recognized as the primary targets for the consumer goods advertised through Zee's commercials.

However, I would argue that Zee TV-Europe, particularly through its programmes like *Your Zindagi* and *Euro Zindagi*, addresses a version of European identity that is located away from and which counteracts the racist and exotic caricatures of South Asian lives towards more eclectic compositions of South Asian identities *in* and *of* Western Europe. By drawing on an array of South Asian news, dramas, soaps, films, sport, and current affairs programmes the range of televisual styles and aesthetic address enhances and makes visible and audible viewers' affiliations with routes across the diaspora – locally, nationally, regionally and internationally.

Since the time of the qualitative research used in this chapter, including the analysis of the two programmes that this chapter has drawn upon (since late 1999), a number of developments have occurred in and on the Zee TV media landscape. These raise a number of interesting and related points for further discussion beyond the remit of this chapter. It is worth outlining them as areas for further work.

First, the Zee TV network in Europe has now diversified into five main channels: Zee TV, Zee Music, Zee Cinema, Z Café, and Zee Alpha Punjabi. The first four in particular continue to broadcast predominantly Hindi language programming. The Zee Alpha Punjabi channel broadcasts its programmes primarily in the language of Punjabi. This latter channel is part of the umbrella group of Zee's Alpha regional channels from South Asia that also include Alpha Gujarati, Alpha Marathi, and Alpha Bangla. The Zee network is obviously keen to capitalize on the variety of linguistic and cultural traditions within South Asia and its Diasporas. Interesting research could be undertaken into the question of whether Zee's operations in the subcontinent allow for as much variety in identity formation as does Zee TV-Europe. For instance, do the main Zee TV Hindi channels include a wide range of Indian representations and identities in an inclusive sense, or is this a function that the regional channels are expected to fulfil in their operations? If the latter is true then is Zee TV in South Asia open to charges that it is reinforcing a north Indian Hindu socio-cultural and political hegemony?

Second, alongside the broadcasting of Zee TV in Europe as well as elsewhere, a number of other channels have come and gone on-air over the past decade or more as part of other media networks. Among those currently broadcasting in 2004 these include: Sony TV (Sony TV Asia), the Bollywood 4 U network (B4U Movies and B4U Music), the Star TV channels (Star TV and Star Plus), ARY Digital, Ekushey TV, PTV Prime, and the South for You channel. The following channels such as Channel East, and the Reminiscent television network (RTV) after being on-air for a year or two have had to withdraw their services due to the lack of sustainable viewer subscriptions and competition from the former channels.[12] Highlighting this fast-changing mediascape in relation to Zee TV alerts us to the intense competition between the different channels that are vying for similar South Asian audiences and advertising revenues.[13] In the context of the channels now off-air, it would be worth asking whether the diasporic Asian media market is able to sustain several broadcasters all at once. In particular, what does the saturation of such television channels into distinct viewer constituencies mean for the development of diasporic South Asians as a social collective?

Third, this chapter has not addressed some of the more exclusive and conservative local and global South Asian identities, particularly as they are represented and constructed through the media of South Asia and its diasporas: including 'fundamentalist' religious identities and right wing diasporic political identities such as the transnational BJP movement. Their relationship with the open communities addressed by Zee TV may produce a tension between the community that is imagined by Zee TV for commercial purposes and the traditional and geographically specific ethnic, religious, linguistic and political differences between the various component social groups of the term.

Meanwhile in 2011, Zee TV in Europe is now in its seventeenth year of operation. It has supplemented the popular cultures of British Bhangra music (Huq; Dudrah 'Drum n Dhol') and Bollywood movies (Gokulsing and Dissanayake) as a recognized and established mode of expression for those South Asians that partake as its audience. Moreover, at the time of writing Zee TV's broadcasting across Africa and the US is well into its twelfth year of operation suggesting its growing popularity in the lives of diasporic South Asians more globally (Joshi). This latter development further illustrates the Zee TV network's rapid expansion amidst the increasing deregulation of the international audiovisual spheres. Ultimately produced for profit, these channels also offer, as we have seen, ways to imagine diasporic identities that South Asian viewers in Britain and elsewhere in Western Europe find convincing, useful and recognisable.

Notes

1. This is a revised and updated version of a previously published article that appeared as Rajinder Dudrah, 'Zee TV: Disaporic non-Terrestrial TV in Europe', *South Asian Popular Culture* 3.1 (2005): 33–47.
2. Naficy develops his theorization of 'epistephilia' by drawing on the work of Bill Nichols. Nichols used the term originally in his discussion of documentary films to describe the process of how viewers draw pleasure through social engagement rather than sexual pleasure, which is characteristic of discussions of fictional narrative cinema.
3. I use the formal corporate name 'Zee TV-Europe' throughout this article to outline the specific workings and reception of Zee TV in the UK and Western Europe in distinction to Zee TV operations in South Asia, albeit Zee TV-Europe broadcasting its logo as 'Zee TV' thereby known by its European viewers as Zee TV. Zee TV-Europe broadcasts from its studios in Northolt, Middlesex in West London.

    In contrast, Zee TV in South Asia is much bigger in terms of its audience reach and corporate structure comprised of its two sister channels Zee Cinema and Zee India. Together the three channels are corporately known as Zee International (see Wanvari; Ray and Jacka). Since 1999 Zee TV has launched a range of further channels under the Zee Alpha label and they are Alpha Bangla, Alpha Gujarati, Alpha Marathi, and Alpha Punjabi. These channels are niche marketed according to language and region within South Asia (see conclusion of this article for a further discussion of these and other non-terrestrial South Asian channels).
4. However, the article also recognizes the debates that have occurred in contemporary Black British political identities. For instance, some academic commentators have called for the assertion of the political term Asian over Black (see Modood; Modood 'Political Blackness'). The debate engendered by such commentators entails whether it is feasible to categorize people of South Asian and African and Caribbean descent within an inclusive Black definition due to the complexities in geographical, cultural, and social affiliations. Others have commented that it is by no means clear that people who are designated Black by political activists and academics consider themselves in these politicized frames of reference (Mercer). Thus, whilst acknowledging the shifts that have occurred of late in debates over Black Britishness this article contends the importance of a continuum of Black political identities as opened up by new forms of identification, arguing for simultaneous and multifaceted positions which are Asian, Black, and British in the cultural and political fields. Rather than simply replace Black British with British Asian struggles, in an easy culturalist and ethnic absolutist sense, it is argued that the struggles of different non-white people in staking a claim of belonging and advancement in Britain are far from exclusive: often they are one and of the same.
5. Attacks on South Asians and Muslims in particular have also been on the rise since 9/11.
6. There are five mainstream terrestrial channels on British Television: BBC1 and BBC2 are licence funded by viewers, and ITV, Channel 4, and Channel 5 are commercially oriented.
7. The work of Ross (1996, chapter 5), for instance, is an excellent historical account of the emergence and struggles of Black programmes on mainstream British television from the 1950s to the early 1990s. The way in which mainstream television responded to the supposed needs of Black communities must be understood in the specific historical context in which they originated. For example, a policy atmosphere that was dominated by the race-relations issue in which 'race' not racism was seen as the problem and Black communities were thought to be in need of assimilation into the white British way of life. Issues of poor representation and

lack of access to the means of media production were at the forefront of demands from Black communities and campaigning organizations who argued for change. As Karen Ross puts it, '[p]ublic service broadcasting, so called, became the target for dissatisfaction and viewed as part of the same oppressive structure which operated against black autonomy in the real world' (Ross, 120).

See Gilroy for a fuller outline and critique of mainstream programmes during the eighties in terms of a wider 'multicultural' agenda adopted by British broadcasting stations which sought to represent Black issues as a province of each channel's Multicultural Department or programming but not as mainstream British television.

8. See for instance *India Today* 30 March 1998, p. 24, for a profile of Subhash Chandra, rated as fourth richest Asian in Britain with personal assets of £450 million.
9. The name given to the popular Hindi cinema from Mumbai (formerly Bombay), India.
10. Interestingly, the Zee TV-Europe schedule is available on Zee Text (accessible on television sets throughout Europe with Teletext service provided by the non-terrestrial channels), in the British South Asian popular press in the UK, and some national and local mainstream newspapers throughout Europe. These listings further provide access to the channel's pan-South Asian European broadcasting for its viewers on the continent as the broadcasting schedule is the same right across Western Europe.
11. Interviews were conducted after the use of an initial questionnaire survey that was used in a conscious attempt to identify respondents who wished to be identified further. Extracts from the three interviews used in this article were conducted during the summer months of 1998. Admittedly, the interview data used in this article is small. However, this article offers the beginnings of a project that seeks to elaborate on diasporic media forms that are used to construct diasporic identities. Others are invited to continue where I have left gaps or offered partial results. The respondents, under pseudonyms, as they appear in the article are:

    Mozibur, 24, male, postgraduate student
    Mozibur stated during his interview that he is an 'avid watcher of Bollywood films'. He often visits the Asian-run Bollywood cinemas in Birmingham, as well as watching films on Zee TV at home and on video. He also enjoys watching mainstream Hollywood movies as a parallel cultural activity but prefers Bollywood films. He watches Zee TV almost every day, 'dipping in and out of programmes'. He especially enjoys watching the news and current affairs programmes on Zee as it helps him keep in touch with what's going on in and around South Asia. Mozibur also reads British Asian magazines and newspapers like *Eastern Eye*, and he enjoys regularly watching the BBC1 soap *Eastenders*.

    Bally, 26 years old, female, insurance clerk
    Bally lives and works in Birmingham. Among her other cultural and leisure pursuits she cites 'going to the gym and socialising with friends and family'. She enjoys Bollywood cinema going, and regularly visits Soho Road in Birmingham to buy the latest film music albums and Bollywood magazines. This is in addition to shopping in Soho Road for her general groceries and meeting with and chatting to friends. Bally watches Zee TV almost every day but in particular at weekends when she has more free time. She enjoys the contemporary films and the music countdown shows and especially likes the discussion programmes about Asians in Britain and abroad.

    Rita, 22, female, crime bureau officer
    Rita has lived in Birmingham all her life. She enjoys aerobics to keep fit and 'loves dancing to fast Bhangra and film songs at Asian weddings'. Rita said in her interview that she watches Zee TV and mainstream television in 'more or less equal measures'. Zee TV for her is an important channel that helps her 'partly keep in touch with being Asian in Britain'. Among her other cultural and leisure pursuits, she cited going clubbing and buying the latest mainstream European dance CDs as a must for her.
12. RTV, for example, broadcasted a range of channels that were niche marketed for Bengali (Bangla TV), Gujarati (Gurjari), Punjabi (Lashkara), Tamil (CEEi TV), and Urdu (Anjuman) speaking communities in 2001. Additionally, RTV also broadcasted Asia 1 TV that claimed to produce 'entertainment that highlights and creates understanding between Asians from varying religious and cultural backgrounds as a means of bringing together the British Asian population' (www.rtvnetwork.com Asia 1 TV link, accessed 10 May 2001).
13. Interesting of note here are the kinds of adverts that are aired in between programmes on these

channels. Increasingly, cultural and social services (e.g. Black British immigration and criminal law services), and diasporic South Asian products (e.g. sub-continental foods and stores, and retailers such as jewellers) are to be found advertising their brands. In part, this has to do with the competitive rates of advertising offered by the non-terrestrial channels that are much lower in price than their mainstream counterparts and the fact that these channels are viewed as an appropriate vehicle to relay messages to South Asian audiences by consumer services providers.

References

Anthias, Floya. 'Evaluating Diaspora: Beyond Ethnicity'. *Sociology* 32.3 (1998): 557–80.
Appadurai, Arjun. 'Disjuncture and Difference in the Global Cultural Economy'. *Theory, Culture & Society* 7 (1990): 295–310.
Appadurai, Arjun. *Modernity at Large: Cultural Dimensions of Globalisation*. Minneapolis: University of Minnesota Press, 1997.
Back, Les and Anoop Nayak. *Invisible Europeans? Black People in the New Europe*. Birmingham: All Faiths For One Race, 1993.
Balakrishnan, P. 'Tigers in a Prize Fight: Asian TV viewers in Britain'. *Guardian*, (Monday 22 May 2000): 8.
Banerjee, I. '"India" in International Institute of Communications (IIC)'. *Media Ownership and Control in the Age of Convergence*. Ed. Vicki Macleod. London: IIC, 1996.
Chhaya. 'Can Zee Govern the Air?' *India Today*. (18 October 1999): 24D–24F. Harrow: Living Media International Ltd.
Cohen, Phil and Carl Gardner. *It Ain't Half Racist, Mum*. London: Comedia, 1983.
Cottle, Simon. 'Making Ethnic Minority Programmes Inside the BBC: Professional Pragmatics and Cultural Containment'. *Media, Culture, Society* 20.2 (1998): 295–317.
Dudrah, Rajinder Kumar. 'Birmingham (UK): Constructing City Spaces through Black Popular Cultures and the Black Public Sphere'. *City* 6.3 (2002a): 335–50.
Dudrah, Rajinder Kumar. 'Drum n Dhol: British Bhangra Music and Diasporic South Asian Identity Formation'. *European Journal of Cultural Studies* 5.3 (2002b): 363–83.
Dudrah, Rajinder Kumar. 'British South Asian Identities and the Popular Cultures of British Bhangra Music, Bollywood Films, and Zee TV in Birmingham'. Unpublished Ph.D. Thesis, Department of Cultural Studies and Sociology, University of Birmingham, 2001.
Gilroy, Paul. 'Channel 4: Bridgehead or Bantustan'. *Screen* 24 (1983): 130–6.
Gokulsing, Moti K. and Wimal Dissanayake. *Indian Popular Cinema: A Narrative of Cultural Change*. Staffordshire: Trentham Books, 2004 (Revised and updated edition).
Hebbar, M. 'Zee goes to London with a major stake in TV Asia'. *The Asian Age Newspaper* (5 January 1995): 3.
Humphreys, Peter. *Mass Media and Media Policy in Western Europe*. Manchester and New York: Manchester University Press, 1996.
Huq, Rupa. 'Asian Kool? Bhangra and Beyond'. *Dis-Orienting Rhythms: The Politics of the New Asian Dance Music*. Eds Sanjay Sharma, John Hutnyk, Ashwani Sharma. London: Zed Books, 1996.
Joshi, N. 'Signals From Home'. *India Today* (6 July 1998): 24L–24M. Living Media International Ltd: Harrow.
King, Anthony. 'Thatcherism and the Emergence of Sky Television'. *Media, Culture, Society* 20.2 (1998): 277–93.
Malik, Sarita. *Representing Black Britain: Black and Asian Images on Television*. London, Thousand Oaks and New Delhi: Sage, 2002.
Mercer, Kobena. *Welcome to the Jungle: New Positions in Black Cultural Studies*. London: Routledge, 1994.
Modood, Tariq. '"Black", Racial Equality and Asian Identity'. *New Community* 14.3 (1988): 397–404.
Modood, Tariq. 'Political Blackness and British Asians'. *Sociology* 28.4 (1994): 859–76.
Modood, Tariq and Pnina Werbner, Eds. *The Politics of Multiculturalism in the New Europe: Racism, Identity and Community*. London: Zed Books, 1997.
Morley, David and Kevin Robins. *Spaces of Identity: Global Media, Electronic Landscapes and Cultural Boundaries*. London and New York: Routledge, 1995.

Moti Gokulsing, K. and Wimal Dissanayake. *Indian Popular Cinema: A Narrative of Cultural Change*. London: Trentham Books, 2004, revised edition.

Murdock, Graham. 'Citizens, Consumers and Public Culture'. *Media Cultures: Reappraising Transnational Media*. Eds Michael Skovmand and Kim Christian Schroder. London and New York: Routledge, 1992.

Naficy, Hamid. *The Making of Exile Cultures: Iranian Television in Los Angeles*. Minneapolis: University of Minnesota Press, 1993.

Nayak, Anoop. '"Pale Warriors": Skinhead Culture and the Embodiment of White Masculinities'. *Thinking Identities: Ethnicity, Racism and Culture*. Eds Avtar Brah et al. Hampshire: Macmillan Press, 1999.

Nayak, Anoop. 'Racism in Birmingham: Some Underground Oversights'. *Invisible Europeans?: Black People in the New Europe*. Eds Les Back and Anoop Nayak. Birmingham: All Faiths For One Race, 1993.

Nichols, Bill. *Representing Reality: Issues and Concepts in Documentary*. Bloomington: Indiana University Press, 1991.

News Corporation. *News Corporation Ltd Annual Report 1994*.

Ray, Manas and Elizabeth Jacka. 'Indian Television: An Emerging Regional Force'. *New Patterns in Global Television: Peripheral Vision*. Eds John Sinclair et al. New York: Oxford University Press, 1996.

Risaluddin, M. 'Going Global – Zee TV Hits South Africa and USA' *Galaxzee International* 1.2 (1996): 5.

Robertson, R. *Globalisation*. London: Sage, 1992.

Ross, Karen. *Black and White Media: Black Images in Popular Film and Television*. Cambridge: Polity Press, 1996.

Sardou, Florentina. *A Single Currency for Europe: Pros and Cons*. Manchester: University of Manchester, 1999.

Sinclair, John. Elizabeth Jacka and Stuart Cunningham, Eds. *New Patterns in Global Television: Peripheral Vision*. New York: Oxford University Press, 1996.

Singh, N. *Zee TV – Europe: A strategic marketing review of Zee TV – Europe following the acquisition of TV Asia*. Bombay, India: Essel Group, 1995.

Skovmand, Michael and Kim Christian Schroder, Eds. *Media Cultures: Reappraising Transnational Media*. London and New York: Routledge, 1992.

Thussu, Daya Kishan, Ed. 'Infotainment International: A View from the South'. *Electronic Empires: Global Media and Local Resistance*. London: Arnold, 1998a.

Thussu, Daya Kishan, Ed. 'Localising the Global: Zee TV in India'. *Electronic Empires: Global Media and Local Resistance*. London: Arnold, 1998b.

Tololyan, Kachig. 'Rethinking Diaspora(s): Stateless Power in the Transnational Moment'. *Diaspora* 5.1 (1996): 3–36.

TV Asia, 'Welcome to the TV Asia Experience'. TV Asia Press Pack, November 1994.

Wanvari, Anil. 'Outward Bound Chandra Takes Zee TV Global'. *Cable and Satellite Asia* (1996): 11–17.

Zee TV. *Zee TV & You: A New Beginning*. UK: Zee TV Public Relations Department: Middlesex, 1997.

'Beaming it live': 24-hour television news, the spectator and the spectacle of the 2002 Gujarat carnage

Anuja Jain

Department of Cinema Studies, New York University, New York, USA

> Recently, following the November 2008 terrorist attacks in Bombay, the electronic media itself became the story. While many commended the extensive 60 hour coverage of the attacks, a debate soon began around the relentless live coverage, and its effect on the security operations and the government actions. Most importantly there emerged larger questions about the changing ethics and aesthetics of the electronic media in India. My essay proposes to understand this marked shift in the concerns, politics, and modes of representation by the media by looking at the electronic media representation of the Gujarat pogrom of 2002, the first major Indian riots of the 24-hour television age. I argue that it is with the extensive coverage of Gujarat conflagration, the 24-hour news phenomenon forever changed the representation of 'crisis' and its affect within the public sphere.

Introduction

The economic liberalization of 1990s affected two pertinent shifts within the socio-material life of the Indian nation-state – the rapid satellite television expansion, and the rise of the new middle class identity. In less than a decade following the 1990s cable television revolution, beset by the simulating images of the Gulf War pouring in live through CNN, the coming of STAR with its package of Star Plus, Prime Sports, MTV, BBC and American television shows and Hollywood films in 1991, the launch of Zee TV and its Hindi language based programming in October 1992, by the first decade of the twenty-first century the satellite television industry grew to be an almost 300 channel industry, reaching approximately 39 million homes in just 10 years with an estimated revenue of Rs. 500 billion ('Channel Viewing'). Significantly, out of these 106 channels broadcasted news in 14 languages and at least 50 were 24-hour satellite news channels, broadcasting news in 11 different languages (Mehta 1). Operating at an interface of capitalism, technological expansion and globalization while these television channels scoured the skies for satellite space, the dramatic rise of the international private satellite networks offering an array of foreign and indigenous cultural products to millions of Indian households ushered in new concerns around national communication systems, and constructions of 'local' cultural identity.

With the rapid transformations in media ownership and control, the 2000s not only proved to be a watershed in this evolving relationship between the market forces, the new audio-visual medium and its message, but also between the long standing genealogy of sectarian strife and its representations within the public sphere in India. On 27 February 2002 the Sabarmati Express pulling out of Godhra in Gujarat was stoned, and subsequently a coach carrying *kar-sevaks* returning from Ayodhya was set on fire by an irate mob. The passengers were largely supporters and affiliates of Vishwa Hindu Parishad (VHP) returning home after participating in a political rally to mobilize support for beginning construction of the Ram temple at the disputed *Ramjanmabhoomi* – Babri Masjid site in Ayodhya by 15 March 2002.[1] Despite the varying accounts about the identity of the attackers and their motives, the Hindu right called for 'retaliation' against the Muslims.[2] Consequently, there ensued one of the biggest ever pogroms against the Muslims in India, with women and children as the targets of the violence.[3] This moment of murder and mayhem was much reported by both the electronic and the print media with an immediacy and urgency befitting the magnitude of the genocide that Gujarat witnessed. While many commended the extensive 24-hour coverage of the genocide, following Gujarat Chief Minister Narendra Modi's victory in the assembly elections after the genocide, soon a debate began around the relentless live coverage. Both the media practitioners as well as the cultural theorists were faced with the urgent questions about the changing ethics and aesthetics of the electronic media in India. My essay analyzes this marked shift in the concerns, politics, and modes of representation that informed the electronic mediations of the 2002 Gujarat genocide, the first major Indian riots of the 24-hour television age. I interrogate how the extensive coverage of Gujarat conflagration, the 24-hour news phenomenon, forever changed the representation of 'crisis' and its affect within the public sphere in India. The essay address questions about the mediation of suffering, the ways in which, informed by the changing social practices, politics of economic and urban restructuring and rampant techno-capitalism, satellite television uses new media technologies, and the possible implications of the discourse for its intended spectator. As I articulate the relation between transnational media forms and their socio-political context, I ask: what are the implications of the emergence of the new electronic media genre, and its representation of communalism for understanding the very meaning of the term 'communalism' today? What role does television, especially electronic media, play in re/thinking about the idea and ideals of nation, national identity and secularism in post Gujarat India?

'An ounce of image, a pound of performance' – debates on the role of the electronic media

Many media critics and scholars have criticized the role of the 24-hour electronic media, raising questions about the media ethics, and implications of the new media revolution within the country. Many deem the coverage 'dull and disappointing,' arguing that the broadcasts began commendably with extensive broadcast of the violence from the worst affected areas, and attempted to shake the viewers, especially the bourgeois armchair spectators by repeatedly showing horrific scenes of 'middle class women collecting ammunition for the battle ahead and otherwise smooth-talking, accomplished people driving down their Marutis to loot electronic items from hitherto splendid showrooms' (Salam). However, soon it was the statements of the political leaders and not the actual tragedy, the nature of the violence and its implications that became the lead stories for almost all the channels. The human death and human dimension of the violence became merely statistics. Many others point out that the media was manipulated by the Gujarat Chief Minister Narendra Modi. Television provided Modi with a 'national pulpit' and an 'arena for mass mobilization' (Desai 228–34; Mehta). Even though much of the national media coverage of Modi and the partisan role of his government were negative, Modi used this to underline the radicalism of his political message and play to his constituency.

He managed to remain in the news by constantly issuing controversial statements, and the media constantly chased him everywhere. Constantly iterating that the criticism of his government's handling of the riots was an attack on 50 million Gujaratis and an insult to Gujarati *'asmita'* (pride), in speech after speech he managed to successfully mobilize, and maintain the anger against the national media.

This national-regional manipulation thesis does situate the 24-hour media reportage of the genocide within the evolving relationship between communalism and technology that defined the post liberalization Indian landscape, and suggests the ways in which new audiovisual technologies were being used for the purposes of political mobilization and ideological indoctrination. However, within the same post liberalization landscape it also becomes imperative to situate and analyze the extensive media representation of the carnage within the emergence of a wider national socio-political culture, one that is marked by the shift from the older ideologies of a state managed economy to a middle class consumption culture. This is not to overlook the tenuousness of deterministic structures of popular perception and adequate availability of frames to understand mass media genres like news in the Indian public sphere which is marked by an enigmatically diverse media culture. However, this is to underline the significance of the rapid expansion of satellite television, the emergence of 24-hour television news, and their representational ethics and aesthetics is part of the wider array of visual images and public discourses that have accompanied the economic reforms and policies since the 1990s, and are constitutive of as well as constituted by the shifting role of the middle class, their attitudes, lifestyles and consumption practices.[4] Henceforth, my essay argues that the analysis of the electronic media representation of the genocide should be examined as a complex discursive formation, situated within the nexus of the economic liberalization that first began in Rajiv Gandhi's regime in 1980s and has since expanded through the 1990s period of economic reforms, the new identity constructions of the urban middle classes and their patterns of commodity consumption, globalization and technologies of mediation that came to inform the Indian social and political life at the time of Gujarat pogrom. The emergent new moral order following liberalization was one where consumption was no more 'a social act in a specific sense; the individual had to be mindful of national constraints, avoid waste, and refrain from self-indulgence' (Rajagopal 'The Public Sphere' 14). With government policies increasingly promoting middle class consumption, new forms of commodity consumption appropriate for urban lifestyle became patent and consequently so did new identities, such as those one could call *consumer-spectator*.

In the post liberalization landscape, right from the emergence of multiplexes as an exclusive space within the historically contested public space of the cinema hall, intended and consumed by a privileged social group, the desire for the management of public space also extended to urban restructuring and constitution of new civic cultures for the middle classes through beautification projects undertaken by resident associations and civic organizations in various neighborhoods in metropolises like Mumbai (Fernandez 2415–30). The production of middle-class identity was growingly linked to a politics of 'spatial purification' which 'centers on middleclass claims over public spaces and a corresponding movement to cleanse such spaces of the poor and working classes' (Fernandez 2416). Creation of such urban aesthetics was informed not only by strict class based separations, but it constituted the new public culture where consumerism was not merely circumscribed to material consumption, but also extended to a new form of visual consumption. It was the consumption of an excess, the spectacular and its sensational pleasure – the bright street lighting of urban gated communities, the opulent houses, huge billboards on the roads, popular Hindi cinema with its new visual landscape where there were neon lights in the background, glossy beverage brands and palatial designer homes in the foreground, foreign automobiles and locations everywhere, the expensive shiny glass structures of the shopping malls, and the glittering shop windows with their attractive mannequins. These new practices of looking constituted a new *consumer-spectator* who growingly comes to inhabit a world that promises constant transitory high intensity stimuli, and informs a public sphere which is selective and rigidly class defined, 'one which defines the individual through their consumption, and gives them a sense of belonging' (Shah 5).

Constituted and constitutive of this leisure culture and dynamic media economy was also the expanding satellite television, its many texts and images. It was another medium directed at the new social group, and was a key facilitator in new trade of images defining the contours of the transforming relationship between modernity and middle class citizenship in the Indian society. Unlike Doordarshan which primarily still 'attempted to reach out to the masses – and even the rural masses who can't afford TV sets – with a bizarre mix of programming that satisfies nobody,' satellite television was definitive about its target audience (Sanghavi). As Sanghavi further points out, 'because the money comes from advertising, and because advertisers are only interested in people who are affluent enough to afford their products, most commercial television is directed at the middle class' (Sanghavi). Thus it was this middle class consumer-spectator in/formed by a consumer capitalism that had finally succeeded in weaning him away from a 'strongly entrenched culture of thrift towards a system of gratification more firmly in its (capitalism's) own long term control' (Prasad) who was the intended audience of the extensive 24/7 reportage of the genocide. Moreover, as my discussion of the electronic media representations would explicate it is this *consumer-spectator* who is at the centre of a new interface of media, politics and market, and has resonating implications for representations of 'crisis' and their affect.

'Beaming it live': 24/7 phenomenon, the spectator and the spectacle of the 2002 Gujarat carnage

Within the genealogy of sectarian strife that has always been fraught by concerns and debates over the representation of emotive and communally charged moments of strife and mayhem by the televisual apparatus, long standing state monopolized news culture and consequent censoring of images and idioms of communal strife, the 24-hour news channels emerged as one of the most popular and propelling agents of the extensive satellite TV expansion, with particular implications for 'crisis' and the context in which it is mediated and understood. The extensive 24-hour news reportage of the Gujarat genocide was unambiguously marked by intent to lend visibility to the violence, and show the failing of the nation-state.

Being the first major Indian riot of the 24-hour television age with no prolific precedents within the Indian media, taking its cue from the American model of September 11 media broadcasting, and informed and informing the public culture marked by a rampant ecology of images and use of new image technologies, the reportage was incessantly marked by a deluge of images of violence: brutally wounded victims, weeping orphaned children, abused and raped women, debilitated houses and other spaces with traces of human blood and amputated limbs. The attack on the World Trade Centre is said to be the most photographed disaster in the history, producing a spectacle for a city designed to look at itself from spectacular vantage points. The spectacle of 9/11 which was incessantly photographed and consumed globally was the ultimate 'Kodak moment' providing 'flashbulb memories' to those who were not present at the site of the attack, but were allowed a powerful sense of having been present for a momentous historical event

(Kirshenblatt-Gimblett 14–16). The catastrophe witnessed the relentless proliferation, saturation, circulation and memorialization of the images and the accompanying trauma. In the Indian context, on the one hand 9/11 was the point in case for BJP leaders like Advani to critique the relentless electronic media representation of the murder and mayhem in Gujarat, asking the media to take lessons from the American coverage of September 11 2001 and suggested that 'sometimes speaking the truth may not be an act of responsibility' ('BJP builds Bush shield for Modi'). On the other hand, it was an influential benchmark for the electronic media to model its representation of its own moment of monumental catastrophe. They saw it as an example where they followed the American media organizations in the way they lent extensive coverage to the attack, and the accompanying trauma of loss.

The incessantly streaming images of the violence, narratives detailing the human and material destruction commendably created the requisite urgency and immediacy, especially in the face of the censorship practiced by the national Doordarshan channel, the ban on Star News and its reportage by the Gujarat chief minister Narendra Modi and the biased and inflammatory representations by many local Gujarati language news bulletins. The reportage did not let the Indian nation-state simply drift into a state of emergency without bearing responsibility for the failure of its various institutions in taking prompt and adequate steps in preventing the month-long murder and mayhem. The traditionally 'munificent neutral state' could not presume its long standing (supposed) authority to guard against all real and imagined crises, and secularism as a state-led exercise, bouldered by a neutral and secular centre, came under severe crisis (Rajagopal 208–24; Pandey 157–76; Prakash 177–88).

However soon one began noticing a shift in the focus – the shock factor, the immediate, the dramatic were no longer merely the strategies, the performative and narrative idioms borrowed from the popular to create an atmosphere of discomfort, a climate of conscience and engage the viewers – but they became the very ideological predilections of this new media. For instance, on 1 March, as the news reporter on Zee relays for us the raging violence from a particular small slum, in a frontal shot framing him he informs us that there were 150 houses in the area and all have been burnt. He further tells us that some houses were set on fire on the morning of his report. At this point he dramatically pauses and the camera rapidly zooms to a burning house with an accompanying sound effect that mirrors the abrupt zoom and exaggerates its sensational nature. The camera cuts back to him and he informs us that they can still smell the burning flesh. Thereafter follows a series of rapidly cutting wide angle shots of the dilapidated properties and burning homes going back to the news reporter informing us that the police have not been successful in controlling the rioters until now, followed by more fast paced shots of burnt interiors, corpses, wounded people. It is then intercut again with the 2 March archival footage where a different news reporter informs us of a similar incident at another place where many families have left their homes, and then tracking shots of the interior spaces of the destroyed properties with the voiceover giving us the death toll, concluding with shots of Modi and excerpts from the controversial speeches he made. Despite the differing ideology determining the decision to identify the perpetrators and the victims as Hindus and Muslims by the English language Star News and the reversal to the old media practice of not identifying the religious affiliations of the victims by the Hindi language Zee News, the reportage on both the channels was informed 24/7 by the repeated relay of such montages composed of grainy fast paced images of the mayhem continuously drawing attention to their live-ness, self referentiality and spectacular gore. Soon 'repeatage' began replacing the reportage and there followed an 'impoverishment of discourse, both visual and explicative, that results when the media reinforce key images to the point of banality, or replay unexamined clichés to package a difficult situation in a semantics of simplification' (Hoskote 5).

Before I analyze the reportage further, it is important to note here that despite a largely similar aesthetics informing the Hindi and English reportage, there were significant instances of a kind of uncertainty informing especially the Hindi media reportage. For instance, in a 28 February panel discussion when heavy violence marred Gujarat, one of the panelists, Chandan Mitra, the chief editor of *Pioneer* remarks that this violence is because of the 'high running emotions and anger on both sides after Godhra'; the reporter immediately refutes any suggestion of the 'retaliation' theory, and points out that from the reports they have been getting this is not a case of 'rioting' – the Godhra incident is separate but this seems to be an 'organized one sided ostracization of a particular community.' In the same breath as he goes on to iterate the failure of the Gujarat state in taking timely steps to prevent the violence and insists that we should not see it as a 'Hindu–Muslim conflict' despite people trying to give it such an illusion; he also emphasizes that the Zee channel believes that it is the 'conspiracy' by some 'outsiders' and their 'pawns can be people of any religion.' Even in the later instance of naming the religion of the communities, the position of Zee News was asymmetrical. To begin with, in response to BJP Law minister and Rajya Sabha member from Gujarat, Arun Jaitley's accusation that electronic media needs to follow the lead of print media which has always done 'subdued reporting of such communal riots' and has abstained from showing enraging images of burnt bodies, corpses and never identified the religious identities, the news reader immediately responded that if the Zee channel has not done good work then he should openly say so or else 'acquit the channel of any accusation.' Such an anxiety on part of the reporter is indicative of not only the newness of the medium, attempts to define its code of ethics and politics as it responds to the first carnage of this magnitude in the 24-hour age, but the fissured nature of the reporting also articulates the uncertainty that especially informs the Hindi electronic media's endeavors in re/defining its relationship with the ideal of the nation-state which 'now exists as a powerful and tangible material' (Pandey 'The Secular State' 167), and rethinking the role of religion in the Indian society given the altered inclination of this state. The same channel later goes on to identify the religion of the victims and the perpetrators, points to the organized nature of the violence, to yet again revert back to not naming the communities, and a discourse fissured by conflicting narratives of 'outsiders' being responsible for this 'sudden' genocidal violence, or the excess toxins, neural and hormonal imbalances within human mind as probable reasons while also simultaneously iterating the sociological reasons such as mob mentality, urbanization and political organization of most riots ('The Inside Story,' Zee News, 31 March). The reasons for Hindi media's tenuous position as opposed to English electronic media can probably be best understood by looking at the history of English and Hindi print media's reportage of the *Ram Janmabhumi* movement. Although the logic of growth, consumption and affect of the two mediums in both languages has been historically different within the Indian public sphere, the larger politics of language, the historical cleavage between English and Hindi in India, the long standing deep cultural divisions and social distance between the two languages and the ways in which they came to inflect a 'split public' during the movement can also help us comprehend the workings of the Hindi electronic media in the case of Gujarat genocide. Contrasting the English and Hindi language newspaper coverage of the *Ram Janmabhumi* movement Rajagopal points out that, informed by origins of 'English language as an elite form of discourse in liberal market society,' while the English language media regarded issues of religion as peripheral to their concerns, the Hindi media 'treated it as a relatively familiar, living presence and as a sociological fact within their purview [...]' (*Politics After Television* 160). Given the Hindi press' intimacy with the themes and the sentiments of the temple movement, there was a sympathy in the Hindi media for the movement as opposed to English language press for whom the movement was something 'out there' (160, 162). While the Hindi press' coverage of the movement was implicated within debates about the 'inseparability of Hindu religion from the Indian nation' as opposed to English media's military stance towards the movement informed by the language getting subsumed into 'Nehruvian language of command' and continuing with the 'colonial practice of aloofness and unfamiliarity with local traditions' (16).[5] Significantly for the Hindi print media the 'vernacular was the more muddy, compromised realm whose modernity was uncertain, whereas the domain of English was that of secular modernity proper' (162). While the coverage in the English press was largely limited to political and legal issues, to reactions to court rulings and developments in Ayodhya and in the capital, for the Hindi press, the movement was primarily a social and cultural issue.

What I am suggesting by invoking the differential print *Ram Janmabhumi* movement is not that there were no shifts in the questions around sectarian strife in the wake of print media's engagement with sectarianism to electronic media/tions of conflict in the 24-hour television age. I am not indicating that there have been no transformations in the pre-existing relationship between the language groups, or no intertwining of the politics of religious identity with linguistic identity in the wake of 1990s liberalization, accompanying modernization and globalization. Such a suggestion would be tantamount to overlooking the plurality of Indian media culture and the enigmatically fissured Indian public sphere it comes to inform – be it the transnational satellite television revolution with their influx of English and indigenous language programming, or the phenomenal growth of the Hindi language newspapers, beginning with the mid-1980s and continuing well into the 2000s in the Hindi belt of the Indian nation-state (Ninan 260–77; Friedlander and Seth 188–206). However, as Rajagopal importantly points out in his analysis of the print media's coverage of the movement,

> the Hindi language audience is 'regional' in the double sense – representing only a part of the nation, the 'Hindi belt,' and forming within this apportioning, various overlapping cultural and political sectors. Hindi language newspapers therefore tend to be more numerous and to have a greater number of editions corresponding to the dispersed character or their audience. It is in the Hindi language medium that, arguably, a 'Hindu' consciousness as reasserted so forcefully over the last several years, with extensive organizational groundwork by the Hindu right serving to link different regions one to the other to form a relatively cohesive and self-conscious political force. (*Politics After Television* 159–60)

In the context of Gujarat, the Hindi language electronic media did not definitely play a similar role of iterating 'Hindu' identities and was unambiguously critical of the BJP led Gujarat government. During the *Ram Janmabhumi* movement the media's sympathy stemmed from social and cultural understanding of the movement which essentially saw Hindu religion as part of the Indian national identity. Now with Gujarat seeing how the politicization of religion by the Hindu Right has led to a new politics which is structuring the nation along minority–majority lines, there is a sense that the Hindi media is struggling not only with the reconsideration (and reconstitution) of Hindu religion, but also with identifying the cultural importance of religion *per se* for the Indian identity. The uncertainty does not stem from questioning various belief systems, issues of faith or an ideological belief in the Hindu Right's claim of making Indian Hindu, but from the urgent re/questioning of religion as the basis of 'identitarian' cultural practices, and its relationship with the state in contemporary post Gujarat India. English media probably felt more comfortable in dealing with this crisis as their approach has always been historical – as we saw in their coverage of the *Ram Janmabhumi* movement.

This uncertainty did not originate only from the Hindi media's historical relationship with socio-cultural questions of religion and constructions of Hindu identity as indicated by their reportage of *Ram Janmabhumi* movement, but also stemmed from and extended to English electronic media's rather facile understanding of the implications of Gujarat genocide. Despite using words like 'genocide' to describe the carnage, the media failed to see that the crisis was not solely of a government failing to control murder and mayhem, but of the very reversibility of 'the terms of negotiation between politicized religious/cultural communities,' and between these communities and the state (which itself has transformed into a politicized religious community) which have radically, if quietly 'altered at many junctures in the twentieth and twenty-first centuries' (Pandey 'Secular State' 159). In addition, 'a recognition of this reversibility of liberal conditions is necessary to any rethinking of the requirements of a politics of secularism, pluralism, or pluralist democracy today' (Pandey 'Secular State' 159). The 31 March special report by Zee News on the history of religious conflict in colonial and post colonial India is a point in case. The reporter introducing the report sets up the context by iterating that the routine of sectarian strife began many years before independence. Thereafter the report begins with black and white shots of corpses, burning buildings and people protesting with the voice over informing us that in India the first big riot was in 1713, and it happened in Ahmadabad, Gujarat itself. The narrator goes on to tell us that the occasion was that of the Hindu festival of colors Holi, and communal tensions turned into riots between two communities. He points out that though no one kept an account of lives lost, there have been many such riots that have informed Indian history. Thereafter we get statistics tabulating the number of riots, their years, and communally most sensitive places, among which Ahmedabad is listed as one. From here follows a narration of the genealogy of sectarian strife against the backdrop of images of violence, dislocation and ruin with 1947 Partition, 1969 Hindu–Muslim conflict, 1984 Sikh riots, 1992 Babri Masjid demolition and 1992–93 Bombay riots identified as primary moments of 'communalism.' After another section on seeing neural imbalances in the brain as psychological reasons for such aggressive and violent behavior, the report concludes by informing us, 'Such instances of conflict and jealousy among human beings are not new but can be traced back to beginning of human race. In Christianity Cain killed Abel only because he thought that God was being partial towards Abel.' What is significant about this report and the genealogy it traces is not only the danger of reducing Gujarat to yet another moment of routine violence which has marked the Indian experience over decades, but also an essentialization of communalism and communal riots, with 'riots' assumed as essentially 'transparent and immutable entities around which only the context changes' (Pandey 'In Defense' 41). Though while looking at the sociological reasons for conflict there is an iteration that most riots (like Gujarat) are organized, the larger implication remained that such moments are common in the Indian social life and they are primarily instances of mob mentality, enraged misguided passions which suddenly and temporarily disrupt the democratic and secular regime of the nation-state.

In any attempt to analyze these riots the focus was obsessively on the causes rather than understanding the changing dynamics of riot production, or the role technology and communication had come to play. Paul Brass iterates, 'riots are dramatic productions, creation of specific persons, groups, and parties operating through institutionalized riot networks within a discursive framework of Hindu–Muslim communal opposition and antagonism that in turn produces specific forms of political practice that make riots integral to the political process' (369). However, with the genocidal violence in Gujarat there was no recognition that this act of violence against Muslims was of a different order from numerous other earlier events generally coded as 'communal violence' by the report. The special reports and panel discussions were analyzing at length the reasons behind the carnage, the condition of the Muslim community, impact on children and women who witnessed this violence, and rehabilitation work. However in their attempt to understand the cause and effect of the carnage, it is the detailed examination of the economic reasons behind the targeting of the Muslim community that is the focus. While these reasons are unambiguously important, and play a crucial role in understanding the genocide, with being the focus it 'leaves little room for human agency and human responsibility and becomes a statement about the essential and unchanging ("secular") character of the majority of people concerned' (Pandey 'In Defense' 39). Growingly 'the people' find their place outside history, and there is yet again a danger in reducing the 'crisis' to a moment of 'aberration,' and constructing a reductionist history which continues to play a tired nationalist rhetoric of India and Indians being essentially a 'secular' and 'tolerant' nation.[6] Despite clearly naming the communities and identifying the victims as being Muslim women and children and perpetrators as militant Hindu Right aficionados along with middle class Gujaratis, in most of the reportage the contours and character of the violence was simply assumed, with no need for further investigation of its nature and targets. For instance, in a special report on Zee News on 31 March on the condition of women post Gujarat carnage we hear various women's narratives of victimization – from a Hindu woman's husband becoming a paralytic, to a Muslim woman losing her child and being attacked herself. However, there is a homogenization of victims as simply 'women' with the larger narrative of 'everyone' getting affected by the riots. It is completely lost in such reports that the targets of the violence were specifically Muslim women and children, and it was many Hindu families, including women who participated in violence and attacks on Muslims. According to the International Initiative for Justice (IIJ) December 2003 report, violence against Muslim women was a crucial element of how the massacres were executed. The report points out,

> Rape, sexual assault and humiliation were some of the most systematic and consistent mechanisms for violating Muslims and their communities. Women were stripped of their clothes, gang raped, often publicly, and finally, in almost all cases, burnt or hacked to death. Pregnant women were not only not spared the brutality of rape but also had their abdomens slashed open and their fetus thrown into raging fires. Children as young as 3 years old were sexually assaulted or raped before being burnt to death by the Hindu mobs. One of the survivors of gang rape had the Hindu symbol of *OM* cut out on her head. According to hospital reports, women and men had *OM* cut out on other part of their bodies as well and mutilation of women's breasts was a common feature of the violence. (International Initiative for Justice 5)

It was completely lost that with this pogrom it 'is no longer a question of the efficacy of the state in making good on its promises but of the implications of its "spontaneous" identification with the majority' (Rajan and Needham 8). Without the real understanding of the new state of the state, meaning of this radical shift in its role from a neutral arbitrator to a 'politicized religious community,' the critique of the state sanctioned genocide was merely reduced to handful sensational bytes of yet another 'communal riot' in which people were merely 'pawns'. When the commonly understood sense of the very term 'communalism' could no more fit the description of the violence against the Muslims, with such an ahistorical understanding of the carnage any critique of the state, failure of the democratic and liberal regime, and the complacency of the police also began losing its meaning and import.[7]

Despite tracing such genealogies of sectarian strife, the representations were rendered impersonal not merely by their idioms of reporting but also with a disjunction between the present and the archive of the past that charts the ascendancy of Hindutva, the ideology of militant Hindu nationalism, and furnishes the backdrop to enable an understanding of how Gujarat came to become the laboratory for Hindu *rashtra* (nation). VHP international working president Ashok Singhal infamously termed Gujarat a 'successful experiment' that would be repeated all over India. He pointed out, 'Godhra happened on February 27 and the next day, 50 lakh Hindus were on the streets. We were successful in our experiment of raising Hindu consciousness, which will be repeated all over the country now.' He further iterated how villages were 'emptied of Islam,' and whole communities of Muslims had been dispatched to refugee camps. This was a victory for Hindu society, he added (qtd. in Rajagopal 'Gujarat Experiment'; 'VHP: We'll Repeat Our Gujarat Experiment'). However, the media failed to understand and report the significance Gujarat has had in a long standing contest waged by Hindutava within the Indian polity over the nature of an imagined national community. There was no interrogation of either the silence of corporate Gujarat nor of dangerous forms of nationalism such as what Lord Bhiku Parekh calls 'long distance nationalism' – the role of the Gujarati diaspora in the 'money-order framework of Gujarat economy' and in the 'growth of Hindu Right movements in the state through a steady inflow of funds and ideological support' along with 'fostering a particular brand of ethnic and national identity' (Chattarji 112).

Without any context, the continuing sounds and images of violence, destruction and frenzy began reducing reduction merely to free floating audio-visual sensations that offer stimuli without making any demands on the spectator. For instance, beginning with the second day of heavy violence on 1 March many panel discussions on Zee News are prefaced with a montage composed of digetic sound reminiscent of a thriller, a shot of the burning Godhra train, followed by a frenzied shot of people running, being attacked by people clearly wearing saffron stoles around their necks, shops burning and the text in bold red letters reading 'Terrorism's other face.' This montage informed the reporting time and again on the subsequent days as well – be it a panel discussion on the deployment of the army, or a debate among ministers belonging to various political parties about conditions in Gujarat. Significantly not once was there any deliberation or recognition at any point on the images clearly identifying the perpetrators as Hindu Right members. In fact even though Zee News later identified the religion of victims and victimizers for a while before retracting back to not naming them, it largely kept underlining the whole carnage as an act by 'outsiders' and a failure of the intelligence agencies and the Gujarat state government. This discrepancy between the image and the text is not only telling of the fissured asymmetrical reporting by the Hindi language media that I discussed earlier, but is also powerfully indicative of the way in which electronic media was increasingly becoming compromised within the post liberalization consumption culture predicated on the spectacular. All through the montage what we see are not the full screen shots, but what one would call the peep-hole shots where the frame is shaped like an enlarged peep hole through which the viewer is invited to *peep* into this sensational world of violence, and consume the gory images *out there*. Such a framing not only articulates the sensationalism that began informing the reportage, but is also evocative of the lens of the video camera, lending self reflexivity a dangerous new meaning and underlining for the viewer the power of the apparatus, of the new medium that is mediating 24/7 such images right in their drawing rooms. Consequently, for the *consumer-spectator* of post liberalization culture this 'crisis' tended to become yet another good to be looked at and consumed. Just like the images and narratives embedded in consumerism that informed the visual landscape of the new middle class that I detailed in the earlier section, these representations also became embedded in the multiple sources of consumption that clutter their everyday modern experience, fill the public spaces and 'stimulate a shiver of enchantment, a tickle of pleasure,' or a 'recoil of bewilderment – a little burst of feeling' before fading away into blaséness (Gitlin 48–49). For instance, on the third day (2 March) when the whole of Gujarat was still in the grip of violence, a Zee News reporter offers to take the spectator on a tour of violence affected areas, mediated to us through intercutting panning and tracking shots. As he reaches Dariyapur, one of the worst affected areas, at one point the camera stops and zooms to the reporter for the first time who points out that if we get out on the road we will see enough marks of the violence. At this point the camera moves to capture completely destroyed and still burning shops and houses, and the reporter's voice over says, 'such images tell their own story.' Initially it was these very images which conveyed the urgency and the nature of the carnage; however, soon they change into self sustaining and self repeating images robbed of their context, motive and detail, guided by the commandment of speed and obsession, projecting the illusion of confident authority, framed by aesthetics of shock and sensationalism, the representations of the pogrom became images of technological advances, of an excess streaming ceaselessly into a dazzling and seductive Indian information society. By the time the Gujarat crisis happened about 300 private satellite channels were already competing for the airtime of about 40 million Indians having access to satellite television. The reportage signaled an onset of a severe crisis within the media – a crisis of over-stimulation and exhaustion.

The focus of the reportage gradually began being largely defined by *what is seen* and on *looking*, transforming the trauma and violence into a spectacle of suffering, a media manufactured master narrative of 'us' (the media) versus them, chief minister Modi and his government where it was the consumption that attained the total occupation of social life, and consequently alienation was generalized, made comfortable, and 'alienated consumption became a duty supplementary to alienated production' (Debord section 42). The electronic media representations were more and more identified by a politics that is distinguished by not being centered directly on inducing *action*, or on questioning the power of the strong, the systematic ostracization of the Muslim community by the Hindu right or on the nature of the ethnic cleansing, but on *observation* – observation of the capacity of the new media technologies where nothing is anymore gradual and faraway but everything is immediate and proximate. Inscribed within this 'nowness' people saw the genocide unfolding before their eyes over and over again. Soon this ubiquity, bereft of any context, historical memory and detail threatened to turn into a mere observation of the unfortunate by the fortunate who do not experience the suffering with the propensity to initiate a 'politics of pity,' which had polarizing implications of creating a binary of the 'fortunate us' and the 'unfortunate them,' and a distance between those who suffer and those who do not share their suffering or do not experience it directly (Boltanski 3). As the French sociologist Boltanski further notes, such politics never poses the question of whether the misery of the unfortunate is justified. Instead it is satisfied with urgency of action to be taken to bring an immediate end to the suffering (4–5). Along with the distance induced by the succession and fragmentation due to the generalized self repeating images of anonymous mass of people and sensational narratives, media reportage largely had a tendency to produce merely the emotion of pity as opposed to empathy, anger or action.[8]

Temporal dimension of television is often informed by 'nowness,' 'insistent presentness,' 'celebration of instantaneous,' the moment, thriving on its own forgettability and erasure of memory and history (Doane 269, 274).[9] In the case of Gujarat, the representation of crisis also came to be contextualized within this pervasive ideology of live-ness, and the spectators consumed the crisis for and within its impressions of instantaneity, without a memory trace. News much like other mass media often focuses on the immediate, the 'newsworthy' due to its political, ideological and material nature. With the growing significance of mediation and its effects in the public sphere, the interaction of various mediating processes with the technological and social processes, the continuing politicization of religion and community identities in post colonial India, it became imperative for the electronic media to concentrate beyond the immediate, especially in such moments of sectarian strife. However, despite the extensive reportage there was an exclusive focus on Gujarat, and as I explicated earlier the only references to previous historical moments of Hindu–Muslim strife, both in the nation-state and Gujarat were redundantly normative. As during the previous moments of sectarianism, even during the Gujarat conflict the Hindu Right was yet again evoking the historical memory of Hindu–Muslim conflict. Its militant communal discourse has always constructed a memory of these moments to radically distort history and incept the 'myth' of a 'continuous thousand year struggle of Hindus against Muslims as the structuring principle of Indian history' (Basu 47, 2). There has been a constant inscribing of these past moments of conflict into instances of Muslim perpetrated violence. Hindu nationalists have continually insisted that the communal violence confirms the 'evil,' 'threatening' and 'dangerous' character of the 'other' community. Commenting on the Chamanpura incident where former MP Ahsan Jaffery was burnt alive along with 19 relatives, Modi significantly said, 'Investigations have revealed that the firing by the Congressman played a pivotal role in inciting the mob.' When asked about what could have lead to the ex-MP opening fire, Modi said, it was 'probably in his *nature*' to do so ('No Let-Up in Gujarat Carnage'). Even the communally biased local Gujarati media constantly constructed the Muslims in Gujarat as 'terrorists,' 'fanatics' and 'fundamentalists' and were constantly commended by Chief Minister Modi for playing 'a decisive role as a link between the people and the government' by supporting the state government in the 'measures' taken by the government be 'effective and restore normalcy' in the wake of Godhra incident.[10] In another instance making the link between Pakistani Muslims and Gujarat's Muslims, Gujarat health Minister Ashok Bhatt remarked, 'Godhra has a notorious reputation [...] We suspect that many Pakistanis live here illegally.'[11] By foregrounding the 'retaliation' or 'spontaneous rioting' logic, the Hindu right was yet again evoking and mobilizing a fear psychosis by insisting that the entire nation-state is 'populated with "lieux de memoire" that signify the violence done by Muslims to the Hindu body, the dangers of the Muslim populations that reside in the midst of Hindus in cities and towns, and Muslim institutions that teach Muslims to become traitors, all of which must be reformed, replaced or extirpated before India can become whole, united and powerful' (Brass 36). Thus bereft of alternative memories and context that counters such Hindu right constructions, and offers the spectator a landscape to engage with Gujarat carnage by making crucial associations and distinctions with the past instances of Hindutava as well as state perpetrated violence, a distance was affected by the media idioms and narratives that induced an uncertainty of moral responsibility, and the spectator merely either averted his gaze or went on *looking*.

In conclusion I should like to point out that this shift within the media representations raises urgent larger questions about contemporary electronic media's capability to negotiate with conflict when its texture and mediation continues to change within a post liberalization landscape which has become the site of rapidly expanding media technologies, intensifying the ecology of media images and spectacle form of media culture. We are confronted with the immediate question – have the questions around communalism themselves changed with 24-hour electronic mediations of sectarian strife? What do we learn in the wake of this shift from sectarianism to electronic media, and sectarianism within the genealogy of sectarian strife? With the new media representations of sectarianism, the conflict got embedded within a structure of 'crisis,' where critique was its other. Etymologically crisis stems from the Greek *Krisis*, or decision and shares the same root with critique (*Krinein*). Both crisis and critique mark a decisive moment, culmination of a process of weighing, reflecting and arriving at judgment. However, posing an opposition between the 'two etymologically twinned but actively opposed phenomenon' Hoskote points out that, 'where crisis denotes the forcing of an individual decision by structural compulsions, critique connotes an autonomy of decision, a power of reflexive agency on the part of an individual' (3). Traditionally, despite operating within a constantly fluctuating landscape of social, political and cultural determination, media practice was able to negotiate between the two phenomenon – 'the slowness of media technologies meant that there was time to assimilate the shock, to savor the drama in its nuances of dear, trepidation and anxiety, to absorb the textures of crisis and prepare for its denouncement' (Hoskote 2). However today, with the guiding principle of immediacy, ubiquity of sight and accelerated amplification, dissemination and consumption there is a condensation of temporality for both the medium and its spectator. Crisis demands resolution within a limited period of time – 'it compresses time and makes its limitations acutely felt' (Doane 270). Most importantly, crisis invites immediate resolution as the only *singular* closure, and the electronic media by defining the holocaustian politics and violence within such structure of 'crisis' embraced the idioms which 'do not complicate themselves by engaging fully with the issues under review,' but instead are satisfied with urgency of action to be taken to bring an immediate end to the suffering (Hoskote 3).

Identifying with pragmatics that 'embodies decision-making in the form of resolution, however arbitrary,' media debates on sectarianism, national identity and secularism had regressive polarizing implications (Hoskote 3). On many of the talk shows like Star News' 'We the People,' 'Big Fight,' and Zee News' special panel discussions, as the focus shifted from a month long reportage of the violence to deliberation on rebuilding Gujarat, rehabilitation efforts, crisis in BJP ideology, governance and identity, there was an accompanying focus on actively engaging with the issue of secularism, and implications of the carnage for the Indian democracy. While in these debates and discussions it was constantly recognized and iterated that it was a state sponsored riot, within the extensive deliberation on its meaning for secularism and pluralism, soon this space got embedded within a dangerous public memorialization of grief, and a comfort culture of a nation building project. One witnessed the imagination of a dangerous and retrograde form of secular nationalism with an insistence that the solution to this 'crisis' lies in coming together as 'Indians.' For instance, on 2 March, in one of the panel discussions on Star News' 'Big Fight,' Congress leader Kapil Sibal, Samajvadi Party leader Shahid Siddiqui, and Rajya Sabha BJP MP Narendra Mohan are invited as panelists to debate the future impact of Gujarat on Indian politics. As the bickering and the blame game about ownership of sectarian politics continues, the host reporter continuously insists that all parties need to rise above such mudslinging, and the emphasis today is on 'reconciliation – need to come together as *Indians*.' In another 29 March Star News special report, 'Gujarat: Setting an Example' there is an iteration of the 'shining example' of Rustampura in Gujarat where Hindus and Muslims have been living peacefully. Across channels, one continually witnessed the transformation of the Gujarat question into the question of hegemonic national identity, facilitated by the media (and endorsed by the people) like never before. Significantly, in none of these deliberations was there any questioning of the 'structures of identity and authority that have come to organize the Indian nation-state and its "others" along majority-minority lines' (Prakash 187). Instead it was the imagination of a form of nationalism where the minority's difference is yet again subordinated, and in the suggestions of the national oneness looms a danger of reaffirming the minoritization of the Muslim minority – reinscription of the Muslim community within the secular-nationalist hegemony by leaving unchallenged the assumed centre of majority of the nation (Hindu majority) which is aligned with the state. Thus, while the electronic media played an important role in enacting the shift in the career of Indian secularism by showing to us the altered world of Indian politics, one witnessed its failure in comprehending the changed conditions of struggle for secularism and democracy that accompanies this shift in the post Gujarat India. In/formed by such mode of apprehending Gujarat genocide as 'crisis' that is divorced from critique, situated at an interface of capital, technology, expanding information and entertainment industries, the electronic media came to inform a public sphere marked by an erratic interplay of hegemony and resistance.[12]

Acknowledgements

An earlier version of this essay was presented at the 4th International South Asian Popular Culture Conference, University of Manchester, UK, 6–7 July 2009. The author should like to thank the conference organizers and participants for their interest, feedback and stimulating questions at an early stage of the project.

The author thanks the editors, especially Sangita Gopal for approaching her with the possibility of working on this essay, and thereafter offering her constant enthusiasm and endless patience during the writing process. The author is grateful to Arvind Rajagopal and Richard Allen for reading multiple versions of this essay, engaging in many stimulating discussions, and offering invaluable suggestions at different stages of this project. The author should especially like to thank Gauhar Raza for generously sharing his rich archive of television news footage when most TV news channels and Doordarshan archives turned the author away on one pretext or another. Finally, thanks to Pavan Keshavareddy for facilitating the writing process with food and debates.

Notes

1. *Karsevaks* is a term commonly used to refer to the people who offered their support to *Ramjanmabhumi* movement. It was a term popularized by the Right Wing justifying its *rath yatra*, claiming that *karsevaks* participating in it are people who offer their worship through work. Nandy has pointed out that no such tradition exists in Hinduism, and no Hindu temple has ever been built through *Karseva* (6). These *karsevaks* were primarily militant supporters of the Hindutava ideology, and they were incited by the provocative speeches of L. K. Advani and other *Sangh Parivar* leaders to damage the mosque.
2. To date there is much a debate around the 58 men, women and children that were asphyxiated and burnt inside the S-6 coach of the Sabarmati express, and it being an attack on the Hindu *Karsevaks*. While 30 had been VHP *Karservaks*, 19 of them remain unidentified with no relatives coming to claim the *ex-gratia* compensation for them. One was a Muslim passenger. There is also still much controversy and speculation around the reasons behind the attack, nature of the inflammable material used, and how it came to be poured from inside as the Forensic Science Laboratory report suggested. For a detailed discussion of the genocide, role of police, patterns of violence and its aftermath, see Vardhrajan (*Gujarat*).
3. There is a dispute over the exact number of people killed in Gujarat. Official Government of India figures put the death toll at 763 with another 2400 injured. Voluntary agencies and human rights groups, however, put the death toll at close to 2500 (qtd. in Mehta 276).
4. Leela Fernandes (*India's New Middle Class*) analyses in detail the rise of the new Indian middle class, which she deems representative of the political construction of a social group that operates as a proponent of economic liberalization. She examines the ways in which individuals that either identify or aspire to the middle class attempt to deploy various forms of capital in

four primary fields: the media and public sphere, the labor market, urban neighborhoods, and democratic politics.
5. It is important to note here that it was not the *Ramayana* broadcast that initiated the Hindu nationalism, but beginning in the 1980s the Hindu Right began making organized attempts to mobilize the discourse of a religious nationalism. Charu Gupta and Mukul Sharma (1–20) in their study of the communalization of Hindi print media point out that through the 1980s RSS especially made an organized attempt to infiltrate the media, and any casual survey of prominent newspapers in North India would reveal their growing 'hinduisation' (4). In addition, during the *Ramjanmabhumi* movement, and the subsequent 1992 Babri Masjid demolition, the Hindi language press was especially indicted for playing the crucial role in 'propelling the transition from Hindu symbolism to communal praxis' (Farmer 109). Many studies of the press, and the Press Council of India's investigation, pointed out how 'the overwhelming part of the mass-circulated Hindi press – turned *kar sevak* in response to the crisis' (Farmer 109). The English language press was also accused of providing myopic view of major transformations, without a broader understanding of political structures and processes in India.
6. Here my analysis is informed by Gyanendra Pandey's ('In Defense' 27–55) influential writing on historiography of sectarian violence, especially his discussion of the Bhagalpur riots of 1989 within this historiography.
7. See Pandey (*Construction of Communalism*; 'Secular State') for a detailed discussion of the construction(s) of the term 'communalism' in colonial and postcolonial India.
8. Taking up the contrast between compassion and pity, Arendt argues that unlike pity, compassion has a practical character with no great interest in *emotion* or *feeling*, and is directed towards particular individuals and suffering beings without seeking to develop any 'capacity for generalization' (86).
9. Doane in her discussion of the temporal dimension of representation of crisis, catastrophe and information by television, significantly draws on Heath and Skirrow's work and points out that in comparison to film, television, operates much more as an absence of memory as the recorded material it uses – including the material recorded on film – is instituted as actual in the production of the television image (274–5).
10. 'Thank you, *Sandesh*.' This is a letter sent by the Narendra Modi to the editor of *Sandesh*. See Patel, Padgaonkar and Verghese.
11. Oza qtd. in Vardharajan 7.
12. Defining the Indian Public Sphere, Rajagopal significantly points out that few would accept the Habermanisan argument about bourgeois public sphere as a space enabling individual participation in modern democracy. However, what are important are the questions he posed, and not the answers. Rather than assume that 'modern communication technologies help create enlightened democratic conditions,' Habermas asks: 'what is the relation between a communication form [such as print] and its socio-political context?' (Rajagopal 'The Public Sphere' 2).

Notes on contributor

Anuja Jain is a Ph.D. candidate in the Department of Cinema Studies at New York University. She is writing her dissertation on Indian documentary representations of sectarian violence. She has a Masters and an M.Phil in English from the Department of English at the University of Delhi in Delhi, India. She is the recipient of the prestigious American Institute of Indian Studies (AIIS) Research fellowship for the year 2010–2011. She has published an essay on Hindi popular cinema and Indian documentary representations of sectarianism in the anthology *Narratives of Indian Cinema* (2009). She also has a forthcoming entry in *The Sage Encyclopedia of Social Movement Media* (2010). Her research and teaching interests include Indian cinema and media studies, international documentary film and theory, South Asia, cultural studies, postcolonial theory and criticism.

References

Arendt, Hannah. *On Revolution*. Harmondsworth: Penguin Books, 1990. Print.
Basu, Tapan, et al. *Khaki Shorts and Saffron Flags: A Critique of the Hindu Right*. Delhi: Orient Longman, 1993. Print.
"BJP builds Bush shield for Modi." *The Telegraph* (Kolkata) 7 Apr. 2002. Print.

Boltanski, Luc. *Distant Suffering: Morality, Media and Politics*. Trans. Graham Burchell. Cambridge and New York: Cambridge UP, 1999. Print.

Brass, Paul R. *The Production of Hindu-Muslim Violence in Contemporary India*. Seattle: U of Washington P, 2003. Print.

"Channel Viewing." Editorial. *The Hindu* 20 May 2002. Print.

Chatterji, Subarno. "Media Representations of the Kargil War and Gujarat Riots." *Sarai Crisis Reader*. Ed. Shuddhabrata Sengupta, Monica Narula, Ravi Vasudevan and Ravi Sundaram. New Delhi: Sarai Media Lab, 2004. 110–7. Print.

Debord, Guy. *The Society of the Spectacle*. Trans. Donald Nicholson-Smith. New York: Zone Books, 1994. Print.

Desai, Darshan. "Massacres and the Media: A Field Reporter Looks Back on Gujarat 2002." *Sarai Crisis Reader*. Ed. Shuddhabrata Sengupta, Monica Narula, Ravi Vasudevan and Ravi Sundaram. New Delhi: Sarai Media Lab, 2004. 228–34. Print.

Doane, Mary Ann. "Information, Crisis, Catastrophe." *The Historical Film: History and Memory in Media*. Ed. Marcia Landy. New Brunswick, NJ: Rutgers UP, 2001. 269–85. Print.

Farmer, Victoria L. "Mass Media: Images, Mobilization, and Communalism." *Making India Hindu: Religion, Community, and the Politics of Democracy in India*. Ed. David Ludden. Delhi: Oxford UP, 2005. 98–114. Print.

Fernandes, Leela. *India's New Middle Class: Democratic Politics in an Era of Economic Reform*. Minneapolis: U of Minnesota P, 2006. Print.

Fernandes, Leela. "The Politics of Forgetting: Class Politics, State Power, and the Restructuring of Urban Space in India." *Urban Studies* 41.12 (November 2004): 2415–30. Print.

Friedlander, Jeffrey, and Sanjay Seth. "'Subliminal Charge': How Hindi Language Newspaper Expansion Affects India." *The Indian Public Sphere: Readings in Media History*. Ed. Arvind Rajagopal. New Delhi: Oxford UP, 2009. 188–206. Print.

Gitlin, Todd. *Media Unlimited: How the Torrent of Images and Sounds Overwhelms Our Lives*. New York: Metropolitan Books, 2001. Print.

Gupta, Charu, and Mukul Sharma. "Communal constructions: media reality vs. real reality." *Race & Class* 38.1 (1996): 1–20. Print.

Hoskote, Ranjit. "Bearing Inconvenient Witness: Notes in Pro/Confessional Mode." *Sarai Crisis Reader*. Ed. Shuddhabrata Sengupta, Monica Narula, Ravi Vasudevan and Ravi Sundaram. New Delhi: Sarai Media Lab., 2004. 2–9. Print.

International Initiative for Justice. *Threatened Existence: A Feminist Analysis of the Genocide in Gujarat*. Dec. 2003. Web. <http://www.coalitionagainstgenocide.org/reports/2003/iij.dec2003.report.pdf>.

Kirshenblatt-Gimblett, Barbara. "Kodak Moments, Flashbulb Memories: Reflections on 9/11." *The Drama Review* 47.1 (Spring 2003): 11–48. Print.

Mehta, Nalin. *India on Television: How Television News Changed the Way We Think and Act*. New Delhi: Harper Collins, 2008. Print.

Nandy, Ashis, et al. *Creating a Nationality: The Ramjanmabhumi Movement and Fear of the Self*. New Delhi: Oxford UP, 1995. Print.

Ninan, Sevanti. "Local News Gatherers." *The Indian Public Sphere: Readings in Media History*. Ed. Arvind Rajagopal. New Delhi: Oxford UP, 2009. 260–77. Print.

"No Let-Up in Gujarat Carnage." *Hindustan Times* 1 Mar. 2002. Print.

Pandey, Gyanendra. *The Construction of Communalism in Colonial North India*. New Delhi: Oxford UP, 1990. Print.

Pandey, Gyanendra. "In Defense of the Fragment: Writing about Hindu-Muslims Riots in India Today." *Representations* 37 (Winter 1992): 27–55. Print.

Pandey, Gyanendra. "The Secular State and the Limits of Dialogue." *The Crisis of Secularism in India*. Ed. Anuradha Dingwaney Needham and Rajeshwari Sunder Rajan. Durham and London: Duke UP, 2007. 157–76. Print.

Patel, Aakar, Dileep Padgaonkar, and B.G. Verghese. *Rights and Wrongs, Ordeal by Fire in the Killing Fields of Gujarat*. Ed. Guild Fact Finding Mission Report. New Delhi: Duke UP, 2002. Print.

Prakash, Gyan. "Secular Nationalism, Hindutava, and the Minority." *The Crisis of Secularism in India*. Ed. Anuradha Dingwaney Needham and Rajeshwari Sunder Rajan. Durham and London: Duke UP, 2007. 177–88. Print.

Prasad, M. Madhava. "This Thing Called Bollywood." *Seminar* 525 (May 2003): n.pag. Web. <http://www.india-seminar.com/2003/525/525madhavaprasad.html>.

Rajagopal, Arvind. *Politics After Television: Hindu Nationalism and the Reshaping of the Public in India*. New York: Cambridge UP, 2001. Print.

Rajagopal, Arvind. "The Gujarat Experiment and Hindu National Realism: Lessons for Secularism." *The Crisis of Secularism in India*. Ed. Anuradha Dingwaney Needham and Rajeshwari Sunder Rajan. Durham and London: Duke UP, 2007. 208–24. Print.

Rajagopal, Arvind. "The Public Sphere in India. Structure and Transformation." *The Indian Public Sphere: Readings in Media History*. Ed. Arvind Rajagopal. New York: Oxford UP, 2009. 1–28. Print.

Rajan, Rajeshwari Sunder, and Anuradha Dingwaney Needham. "Introduction." *The Crisis of Secularism in India*. Ed. Anuradha Dingwaney Needham and Rajeshwari Sunder Rajan. Durham and London: Duke UP, 2007. 1–40. Print.

Salam, Zia Us. "Dull and Disappointing." *Hindu* 17 May 2002. Print.

Sanghavi, Vir. "What Star TV Did Not Foretell." *The Telegraph* Jun. 1999. Print.

Shah, Nishant. "Cinema: Reloaded." Mar. 2003. Web. 15 Oct. 2009. <http://hongkongaction.cscsarchive.org/>.

Vardharajan, Siddharth, ed. *Gujarat: The Making of a Tragedy*. New Delhi: Penguin, 2002. Print.

"VHP: We'll Repeat Our Gujarat Experiment." *Indian Express* 4 Sep. 2002. Print.

Muslim punks online: A diasporic Pakistani music subculture on the Internet

Dhiraj Murthy

Department of Sociology and Anthropology, Bowdoin College, Brunswick, USA

> This article seeks to explore how Internet media is shaping transnationally-mediated South Asian music subcultures. Rather than serve as a literature review of new media and South Asian popular culture, this paper is especially interested in how particular music websites, discussion forums, social networking sites, and IP-based technologies in general are facilitating the creation of progressive South Asian virtual spaces. One particular South Asian musical scene, 'Taqwacore', a transnational Muslim punk music scene, is used as a case study. Reference is made to other non-Muslim diasporic South Asian musical scenes including Asian electronic music and Bhangra as well to contextualize Taqwacore. Ethnographic research (participant observation and interviewing) was conducted both online and offline using Facebook, MySpace, Twitter, blogs, discussion groups, and face-to-face meetings.

A diasporic Pakistani student was deciding whether to take a class of mine. The class partially examines diaspora and identity and this particular student was interested in South Asian identities and popular music. He talked about a couple of bands and scenes that he follows – ones I was not familiar with or only peripherally aware of. I carefully scribbled down details. I mentioned to him that we would be studying the significance of contemporary South Asian diasporic musicians ranging from Asian Dub Foundation to Talvin Singh. He similarly scribbled down details. Though an interesting conversation in itself, what particularly struck me was that all of the 'scribbling' consisted of Web URLs (Web addresses). No mention was made of tracks, albums, or record stores who would stock these genres. Rather, the presumption was that a slew of MySpace (a major online social networking website)[1] and record label URLs would do the trick. This was indeed the case as just one of the student's MySpace URLs served as a gateway to several of the diasporic Pakistani scenes he had mentioned.

Of course, there has been scholarship on new media and South Asian popular cultures. However, it is vastly overshadowed by the discussion of matrimonial websites (e.g. Adams and Ghose), diasporic discussion forums (e.g. Mitra 'Nations'), and satellite television.[2] This work, it should be said, was groundbreaking and it has clearly facilitated the academic discussion of new media and South Asia. Working on the Internet in South Asia specifically, Ananda Mitra[3] has perhaps been the most prolific, his research spanning a decade. Though sometimes, but by no means always, gendered and totalizing, his work has, without question, inspired discourse on the Internet and South Asia. In distinction to Mitra, Lal's, Rai's, Gopal's, and Gajjala's[4] work on South Asian diasporic cybercultures have examined the diversity of

South Asian Internet experiences, rather than opting for totalizing constructions of South Asia online, something Adams and Ghose and others fall victim to. South Asian popular culture online includes, but is in no way limited to, Bollywood online (including fan sites, official websites, blogs, and discussion boards), art exhibitions online, Flickr albums, YouTube videos, MySpace pages, Facebook pages, BitTorrent and other peer-to-peer repositories of South Asian music and film files, fashion websites, experimental and traditional South Asian theater, South Asian forums online, and the downloading of South Asian music from iTunes and other online websites/stores (both legally and illegally).

This article seeks to explore how Internet media is shaping transnationally-mediated South Asian music subcultures. Rather than serve as a literature review of new media and South Asian popular culture, I am especially interested in how particular music websites, discussion forums, and IP-based technologies are facilitating the creation of progressive South Asian virtual spaces. I will use this particular South Asian musical scene, 'Taqwacore', a Muslim punk music scene, as a case study, although I will refer to other non-Muslim diasporic South Asian musical scenes including Asian electronic music and Bhangra as well. Taqwacore is an Islamic punk music scene which took its name/inspiration from Michael Muhammed Knight's novel of the same name. The most prominent band in the scene is 'The Kominas', who self describe their music as 'explosive Pakistani punk rock'.[5] Their MySpace presence consists mostly of album track samples and corresponding images from their debut album, *Wild Nights in Guantanamo Bay*. Their music and visual aesthetic, like that of the UK-based band Fundmental's most recent album *All is War*, is a response to post-9/11 and 7/7 Islamophobia. Although my initial entry into the Taqwacore scene was through a physical meeting with my student, my first phase researching it was done purely online (including ethnographic interviews and observation). In this phase, I observed Taqwacore-related Facebook and MySpace pages, discussion groups, and blogs. I also maintained a user account on Twitter.com, a popular social media website, which I used as a conduit for participant observation (at the time of writing, nearly 40 individuals involved in the Taqwacore scene showed interest through Twitter). I conducted virtual interviews by e-mail, Twitter, and Facebook messages. In the second phase of my research, 37 face-to-face interviews were conducted in eight metropolitan US cities.[6] As a way of background, I will first introduce the Taqwacore scene.

Taqwacore

The Taqwacore scene, which Knight fictionalizes in Buffalo, New York, centers on a house shared by a group of 'punk Muslims'. The novel chronicles their negotiation/reconciliation of punk music and Islam. Taqwacore became a sort of self-fulfilling prophecy, with a fictional non-existent music scene giving birth to a real one through bands such as The Kominas, Vote Hezbollah, and Secret Trial Five (an all-women band) to name a few. Vote Hezbollah, the name of one of the bands in Knight's novel, was brought to life by Kourosh Poursalehi, a Sufi Muslim teenager in San Antonio, Texas. In 2004, he put to music a poem at the start of Knight's book titled 'Muhammad was a punk rocker', unwittingly setting in motion the nascence of the non-fictional Taqwacore scene. Poursalehi sent the track to Knight. Around the same time, two young diasporic Pakistani Muslims in the Boston suburbs, Basim Usmani and Shahjehan Khan, had been in touch with Knight, impressed by his novel. Knight visited them and brought along Poursalehi's track. Listening to it on repeat in Knight's car, Khan was shocked that 'there was this kid down in Texas writing this music' (qtd. in Crafts). Khan and Usmani, deeply inspired by Poursalehi, were later to start 'The Kominas', the most recognized of the Taqwacore bands.

Though the Taqwacore scene was initially spawned through physical media (i.e. Knight's book) and physical exchange (i.e. tracks being posted and Knight's trip to Boston), its subsequent growth spurt has been largely mediated by the Internet and IP-based technologies (especially peer-to-peer file sharing).[7] The Internet has been a prime breeding ground for the scene (freely sharing tracks, a process which has virally exposed the scene to like-minded young diasporic Muslims). Furthermore, forums/blogs discussing Taqwacore have enabled old and new scene members to meaningfully discuss both the novel and its offshoot music scene. The Punkistani Live Journal,[8] for example, comments on The Kominas' album and the Taqwacore Forum[9] showcases posts ranging from the scene to a critique of popular Orientalist imagery. In the latter, posts visually critique popular Orientalist essentialism. One post (from March 2008) has a copy of an advertisement for 'Fatima Turkish Cigarettes' with a veiled woman proffering a taste of the exotic Orient with every smoke. Historical and extant popular Orientalism are juxtaposed and contested through new media's ability to embed images. Similarly, the embedding of YouTube videos and music has proved a fertile ground for the anti-essentialist politics of Taqwacore to be highly expressive. Furthermore, the openly activist nature of these particular forums/blogs is reminiscent of early (offline) punk 'zines' (home-made fan magazines). The rough DIY aesthetic of blogs (with images and text sometimes quickly slapped together) often oozes a quasi-punk aesthetic.

Figure 1. E-flyer for a Taqwacore event in Chicago.

'Cybertaqwa'

Whether online or offline, the authenticity (and often this is critical to 'success') of a punk scene depends on engaging with one's fan base through accessible communication mediums (zines were critical to this in pre-online punk movements). However, zines tend to circulate only so far. Usually, they are available at concerts, events, and record stores important to the scene. Historically, this is been an acceptable arrangement for a locally bounded subculture. However, there is not a high enough concentration of Muslim youths interested in Taqwacore in many American urban centers to maintain a scene actively. One of the differences between old and new media forms has been extended reach. In the case of Taqwacore, tracks and event information have circulated far beyond their immediate locales. For example, a Taqwacore event in Chicago in 2007 was predominately advertised by e-flyers (see Figure 1). The audience at the performance included a fair few people outside of the Chicago area. Although alluding to the middle passage, '9000 miles', a track by The Kominas, simultaneously reminds us that the Muslim diaspora is dispersed across great distances (a sentiment doubly reflected by the e-flyer's use of camels).

I have also been particularly struck by the ways in which Taqwacore audiences and artists have reconfigured their traditional roles as producer and consumer. In particular, Web discussion forums, social networking sites, and artist websites have enabled Taqwacore fans to communicate directly with artists. This unique communicative engagement has not only resulted in 'audience' members participating in the production process, but has also enabled 'audience' members to become co-producers. Artists such as Usmani of The Kominas do not shy away from sharing their e-mail addresses. Furthermore, this direct relationship has extended the reach of smaller South Asian musical scenes such as Taqwacore. As such, Taqwacore artists have not had their albums on sale in most mainstream record stores. Rather, fans buy CDs online or download tracks from iTunes or for free from peer-to-peer files haring sites, a process which The Kominas themselves have encouraged.[10]

The multimedia elements of cyberspace (textual, video, photographic, etc.) have been an integral factor in the success of online Taqwacore presences. Social media and social networking websites such as MySpace and Facebook, which I will discuss later, have introduced like-minded youths to one another, a process which has also helped this South Asian musical scene to attract a relatively bountiful membership.[11] Furthermore, Internet-based technologies have facilitated collaborative transnational music-making (e.g. Usmani of The Kominas was living in Pakistan but collaborating with diasporic South Asian musicians in the US). This is not meant to marginalize/downplay the non-virtual, but rather to highlight the significant role of Internet-based media. In particular, Facebook has been instrumental. Though the Internet has been critical in maintaining the scene (through global expansion of its reach and facilitating transnational music-making), the medium has also been integral as an uncensored space for Muslim youths who feel unable to be fully expressive in both mainstream Western public culture (e.g. due to Islamophobia, Orientalism, and exoticization) as well as within dominant Muslim communities (especially orthodox Muslim communities who would consider the scene to be blasphemous).

In the shadow of Rushdie

The publication of Knight's novel exemplifies this role of the Internet. Specifically, when the British printing of *The Taqwacores* was due to be released by Telegram Books in 2006, sections of it were censored for fear of being considered blasphemous or, more worryingly, the harbinger of another Rushdie Affair. Knight reluctantly agreed for those sections to be cut and replaced by an asterisk. The American publisher of the book, Autonomedia, a historically progressive publisher, responded by putting a page on its website showing the censored sections.[12] The British Taqwacore fans printed out this page, which arguably contained the passages that most deconstructed diasporic Muslim identities, and kept it on hand when reading or re-reading the book. For example, in the British version, the following section in square brackets was censored:

> You have to stop trying to make sense of Punk – what it's for, what it's against. It's against everything. [The singer from Vote Hezbollah pissed on a Quran.] Everyone loved it. Then he picked up the kitab, shook some drips off, carefully turned the frail wet pages and recited Ya Sin with absolute sincerity. Somehow the whole thing made sense. (Knight 231)

Post 9/11 and 7/7, diasporic American Muslims have been subject to not only a wave of Islamophobia,[13] but a rampant media-driven portrayal of them as maniacally religious terrorists.[14] This censored section in which one Muslim punk urinates on the Quran simultaneously deconstructs prevalent Muslim essentialisms and offers an alternative vision of one type of new Muslim youth identity. The ability of the Internet to publish the complete, uncensored text from America should not be underestimated in its significance to the British Taqwacore scene, which is just in its infancy now.

Appadurai (15–16) discusses 'culturalist movements', which he sees as the 'conscious mobilization of cultural differences in the service of a larger national or transnational politics'. For him, culturalist movements are usually 'counternational' and 'metacultural'. What he does well is highlight the larger globalized processes, in an epoch of changing mass media, which have affected individual and group 'cultural' identities. However, what is missing from his discussion is how this is occurring in praxis. The censoring of *Taqwacore* and the subsequent Internet response is one example of how the transnational politics of a progressive Muslim youth culture consciously mobilized in aid of its British adherents and how the Internet has supported culturalist movements like Taqwacore.

Transnational South Asian identities online

Mitra's ('Nations and the Internet') study of the newsgroup 'soc.cult.indian' [SCI] was one of the first to examine how emerging Internet-based technologies were mediating the creation of new transnational South Asian cyber-identities. Rather than viewing the newsgroup as a 'little India' online, he emphasizes the divergent as well as convergent ancestries/beliefs/opinions of the group's users. He quotes divisive 'flame' (inflammatory) posts on Muslim/Hindu communal tension (56) as well as ones calling for communal reconciliation (62–63). Although these posts are not relevant to South Asian popular culture *per se*, Mitra's argument that the news group represents a form of transnational South Asian identity, albeit a hotly contested one, is cogent. What Mitra misses however are the nuances of power relations on not only that particular newsgroup, but also the Internet in general. He seems to fall victim to the same cyber utopian visions of Dyson, Gates, and Negroponte[15] in that he believes that the Internet gives 'voice' to everyone:

> dialogue is possible because the space [SCI] cannot be co-opted by any particular point of view. The power and the uniqueness of the dynamics of the electronic community lies precisely in the absence of restrictions and controls on anyone's voice. This is indeed a forum where everyone who is able to access the space is also able to speak within the space. Everyone has a 'voice' in this space. (Mitra 'Nations and the Internet' 67)

The problem in Mitra's analysis is that it conflates the possibility to speak with the ability to speak. The Internet is hardly a space devoid of power relations. Rather, the hierarchies of the offline world frequently manifest themselves in online worlds (Harp and Tremayne 249). Gajjala (14), commenting on Mitra's work, highlights that SCI and other manifestations of the 'cyborg-diaspora' are often complicit in continuing, rather than disrupting, offline hegemonies. Gender is one of the clearest examples of offline hierarchies being transferred to cyber diasporic worlds. Rai highlights how most diasporic Indian cyberspaces take a particular re-inscribed Hindutva masculine identity as normative.[16] This ontological baseline ipso facto not only genders these South Asian diasporic cyberspaces, but also inherently excludes Muslim Indians. This is not surprising given, as Bhatt and Mukta illustrate, the political leanings of many in the Indian diaspora. However, it is a point contra Mitra which needs to be forcefully made.

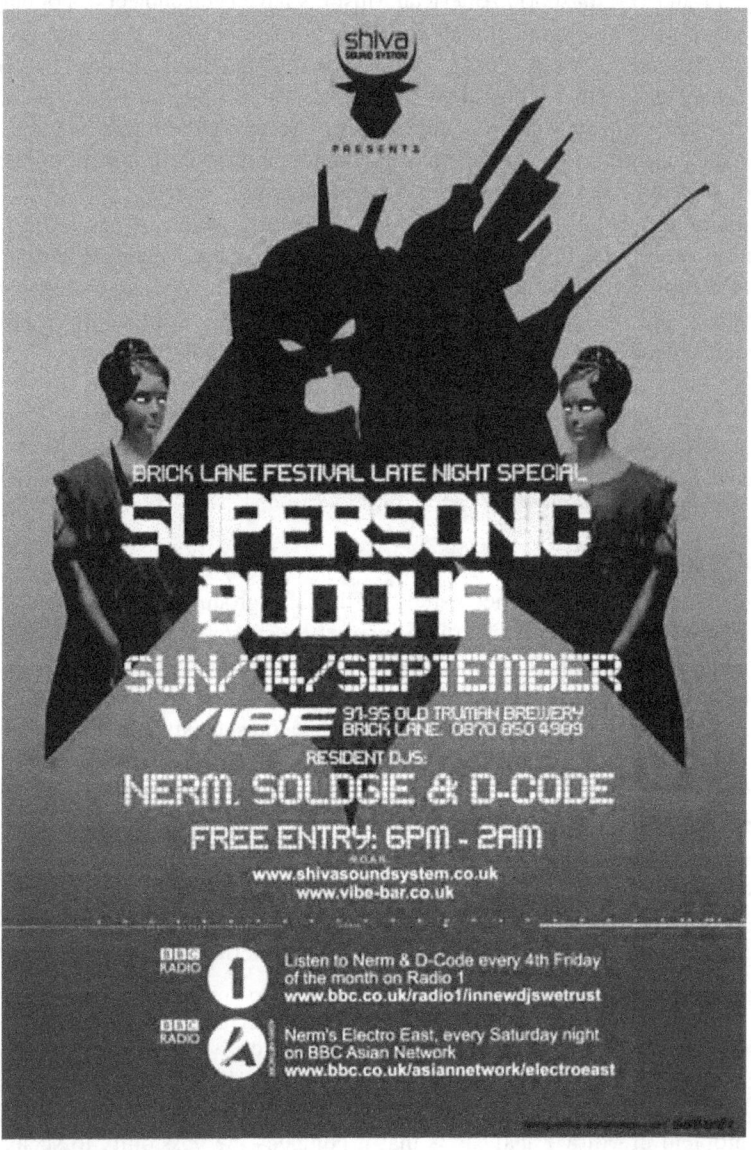

Figure 2. Supersonic Buddha e-flyer.

Though Mitra's ('Nations and the Internet' 66) argument that cyberspaces like SCI 'cannot be co-opted by any particular point of view' is tenuous, his argument that new Internet-mediated transnational South Asian identities – that Gopal ('Home Pages') terms 'a global Indian subject' – can be discerned remains very useful indeed. This is especially true in the case of marginalized South Asian groups such as diasporic Muslim youths, and Taqwacore is a case in point. Basim Usmani's Punkistani blog became a conduit for like-minded Pakistanis, both in the subcontinent and diaspora, to connect. Usmani's own experience highlights of his online interactions shaped his offline interactions:

> My first interactions with sympathetic Pakistanis who I went on to meet afterwards started online.[17]

After The Kominas had gained a measure of success in the US, Basim moved back to Lahore (where he was born) from suburban Boston. He soon met these 'sympathetic Pakistanis' in person and started a new Lahore-based Taqwacore band, Noble Drew. This band also used the Internet to spread their music and its progressive politics. For example, Noble Drew posted a video on YouTube for their track *Thaliyon vi chimero*,[18] which explores the dissonance between state ideology and sexual praxis in Pakistan (including being gay in Pakistan). In Usmani's case, the Internet was critical to the transnationalization of Taqwacore and its politics. He recounted to me how The Kominas' MySpace page attracted punks from Indonesia, Malaysia, and Singapore.[19]

Internet media and transnational South Asian popular culture

Regardless of where one is in the diaspora, new media in its various forms (satellite driven, IP-based, etc.) has enabled the hyper-transnationalization of South Asian subcultures and niche scenes. Taqwacore is only one of many South Asian musical scenes touched by new media in this way. For example, I am a member of several e-mail lists circulated by labels and those interested in the Asian electronic music scene, a transnational South Asian dance music subculture I have investigated elsewhere.[20] I recently received an e-mail from one Asian electronic music list, that of the Shiva Soundsystem, inviting me to a special live Asian electronic performance celebrating the Brick Lane festival in East London. On the flyer (see Figure 2), four URLs are listed. The first is for the record label (a site which includes a discussion forum/blog, downloadable audio clips, and other multimedia materials), the next is for the event's venue, the third is for a related radio program on BBC Radio 1, and the last is for a related radio program on the BBC's Asian Network radio station. The sheer quantity of Web URLs on this flyer is worthy of its own discussion. However, for the purposes of this article, I will draw attention to the significance of how Internet media is encouraging the transnationalization of scenes such as Asian electronic music.

A quick look at the blog discussions on the Shiva Soundsystem not only confirms the transnational membership of those who follow the Asian electronic music scene in London, but also that they use sites including these as key modes of participation/affiliation. Though online and offline participation are qualitatively different, the former is just as immersive and intense, albeit in very different ways such as the inclusion of rich multimedia material. For example, on the Shiva Soundsystem blog, posters frequently embed YouTube videos. A post from February 2008 is illustrative. It has a YouTube video titled 'Little Superstar' embedded,[21] a clip from a 1990s Tamil movie, *Adhisaya Piravi* (also *Adisaya Piravi*) which features Thavakalai break dancing to a remix of Madonna's 'Holiday'. In the clip, the 1980s Tamil megastar, Rajinikanth, uses a tape deck to create a break dance beat. The clip became an Internet hit, garnering over 15 million views on

YouTube alone. Though not obvious, the embedding of the 'Little Superstar' video clip draws viewers into discourse including racial essentialism and crass racism. The clip on YouTube has been heavily consumed and has over 8000 text comments (at the time of writing). The exchange below reminds us of how South Asian popular cultures continue to be racialized, exoticized, essentialized, and othered.

sidscout: That little spick can dance
Tdotspic: I think you mean Indian, ignorant
Naghtora: Fucking Hindus

Similarly, another poster named Irishman182 describes Thavakalai as a 'Muslim Chucky Doll'. The overt marginalization (and demonization as 'chucky doll') of South Asians in the video clip's discussion comments serves not only as a reminder of the alterior position of South Asian popular cultures both online and offline, but its linking from progressive websites/scenes (such as the Shiva sound system blog) offers the chance for counter-hegemonic/anti-racist responses. Scrolling through the numerous responses to Little Superstar, one sees evidence of this, albeit less than we would desire. The lateral connection between the Little Superstar video clip and the Asian electronic music scene is merely one example of how South Asian popular cultures have become exponentially intermeshed through new media forms. These hyperlinked associations also illustrate the potential for diverse South Asian cultural scenes to meet in unforeseen/serendipitous ways.

'Pretty fly (for a white guy)'[22]

One of these ways has been the ability of social networking sites (especially MySpace) to serve as vehicles for non-South Asian fans to participate in South Asian musical scenes. This is definitely, though not exclusively, noticeable in bhangra scenes. There is many a white bhangra fan who feels an unease of being the only non-South Asian at an Ealing, Birmingham, or New York City bhangra (though not 'Basement Bhangra')[23] gig. Notwithstanding discourses of Orientalism, exoticization, and tokenization, there are non-South Asian fans who feel comfortable participating actively online in Bhangra and other South Asian musical scenes. Often, their participation online is enriching rather than diminutive.[24] South Asian diasporic musicians and DJs are well aware of this stereotype. DJ Nerm, during an Electro East BBC radio program exclaims, 'Asian network is not just for brown people'.[25] It is a message at once recognizing and welcoming current non-South Asian participants, but also making it clear to Asian listeners that he believes that South Asian music scenes should not be ethnically endogamous.

This is in distinction to much of the bhangra scene, which has historically been constructed as ethnically South Asian. In the words of one of the lead singers of the British bhangra outfit Cobra, 'Bhangra is Asian music for Asians' (qtd. in Sharma 35). The use of new media by non-South Asian fans of Bhangra is, for this reason, more revealing than within Taqwacore (the event in Chicago mentioned before attracted many white punks) and Asian electronic music (half of whose audiences are usually non-Asians). I was particularly interested in how they were negotiating bhangra scenes (in the UK and elsewhere) online and offline.[26] Predictably, white males were aware that they were being labeled as 'goras'[27] and realized that this awareness had to be made known. Their MySpace pages exemplify this process. Two particular MySpace pages are illustrative.[28] The first is that of Lukas, a 20-year-old male student from Northampton; the second is of Aamil, a 24-year-old Anglo-Indian male living in Patiala, Punjab and working in a call center. Lukas is not only clearly knowledgeable of the bhangra scene (both live and recorded), but also has a good-faith understanding/appreciation of Punjabi culture. Although he does wear a turban, his donning of it does not come off as tokenistic. This is in distinction to the overt exoticization of South Asian popular cultures exemplified by bindi-wearing clubbers, for example (Banerjea 64–79). Lukas' online presence also reveals how some diasporic South Asians have positively responded to him. One of his MySpace 'friends', a South Asian, refers to Lukas in posts as *bhai* (brother). Moreover, out of his over two hundred MySpace friends, many of them are South Asian.

Aamil's background, as self-defined by his MySpace presence, is unique. His grandparents had emigrated from Ireland as civil servants under the British Raj. In distinction to Lukas, Aamil is actually living in South Asia. He was born and lives in India and is 'Indian'. His affinity towards bhangra stems from this rather than from diasporic exposure. Given this, charging Aamil with appropriation or exoticization of South Asian culture is tenuous from the outset. That being said, Aamil's and Lukas' MySpace pages are both similar in their awareness of their whiteness. However, despite their very different backgrounds, they are viewed, prima facie, by some South Asians as interlopers. Their online presences make known their reflexive awareness of their whiteness, but also affirm their appreciation/understanding of bhangra (through sound clips, lists of bhangra artists,

Figure 3. Facebook screenshot of Noble Drew.

etc.). Aamil and Lukas are two examples from many possible ones. My reason for selecting them is that they reveal the ability for virtual worlds to support negotiations of South Asian popular culture which may not always be possible offline.

Desi punks on Facebook

The purpose of social networking sites has been to network friends and like-minded individuals. Though News Corporation's MySpace discussed earlier in this article remains a dominant player, Facebook has recently been more influential in South Asian musical subcultures. Facebook was launched in 2004 and initially relegated to American college campuses (restricted by college e-mail addresses). It was later opened to students of international universities and, in September 2006, to the general public. As of 2006, it had 7.5 million members registered and was rated the top website for youths aged 18-24 (Barsky and Purdon 65–67). By 2007, Facebook had grown to 21 million registered members and garnered an average of 1.6 billion page views per day (Needham & Company qtd. in Ellison, Steinfield and Lampe 1143–68). Like MySpace, Facebook has a separate section for bands to create pages and solicit 'fans' to become page members.

The Facebook page of Usmani's Lahore-based band Noble Drew has been instrumental in extending their fan base. As the screenshot of their Facebook page (Figure 3) illustrates, icons of their fans are listed and those not yet fans are invited to become ones. Usmani recounted to me that over the course of a few days, the Noble Drew Facebook page received more 'fan' requests than his previous band's (The Kominas) MySpace page did over three years, leading him to conclude that 'there are a lot of Pakistanis on Facebook!'[29] If you scroll down the page (an area not pictured in Figure 3), comments from these fans appear on a section of the page known as 'The Wall'. In the case of Noble Drew, Wall posts were posted by fans from Canada, the US, and Pakistan. Besides The Wall, Facebook pages also can contain embedded video (usually hosted at YouTube) and other multimedia content.

As I have discussed elsewhere (Murthy 'Digital Ethnography'), Facebook (and MySpace) enable 'friends' and compound relations (i.e. friends of friends) to network together. Part of this process allows friends and compound relations to see what bands and music scenes their social circle follows. This, in itself, encourages the growth of niche South Asian music subcultures like Taqwacore in that many members of the scene were 'introduced' to it by like-minded diasporic South Asians, a process echoed by many desi music scenes offline.

Though Facebook has been a positive agent of exposure, the ability of new media to reach wider South Asian audiences, though important, has already been well researched.[30] An under-researched significance of spaces such as these is as cocoon, socially protected by the vetting of members and deletion of comments as needed. In the face of violent Islamophobia, it is easier to discuss and distribute Taqwacore material 'privately' online in these secure zones rather than in a shop or at school, leading Usmani to observe that cyberspace can be 'a "safe" place for [Muslim] activists to communicate'.[31] The ability of these spaces, such as the Al-Thawra, Secret Trial Five, Noble Drew, and the (umbrella) 'Taqwacore' Facebook groups, (to at least be perceived) as 'safe' has been alluring to young diasporic Pakistani Muslims who have often felt demonized and otherwise marginalized offline.[32] This cocoon feeling is also partially responsible for the activist sub-topic threads such as 'Muslims in the Media' on the 'wall' of the Taqwacore Facebook page. Gajjala (71), writing about South Asian feminist e-mail lists,[33] similarly found that some list members achieved a 'cozy' rapport, forming 'caucus' subgroups. Mandaville

(146) adds that the ostracization of Muslims in 'Western communities' has encouraged them to go online to 'find others "like them"'.

Conclusion

The presence of South Asian popular cultures in new media is already significant, but continually rising. The explosion of Bollywood-themed and diasporic popular culture websites is case in point. It is tempting to stop at this moment, basking in South Asia's concrete new media presence. However, presence does not always beget position. Moreover, in this case, South Asians continue to be othered/exoticized/otherwise marginalized online and offline. The online presences of Taqwacore and Asian electronic music discussed in this article have been spaces where these marginal essentialisms had been contested. Furthermore, in the face of post-9/11 and 7/7 Islamophobia, 'Taqwacore' cyber-spaces have been viewed as 'safe' outlets for progressive South Asian Muslims to discuss and organize. Though the Internet's role in growing South Asian musical subcultures is important, it is critical not to let this overshadow the role of these virtual spaces as cocoons where South Asian youths (especially marginalized Muslim youths) can express themselves creatively and freely. Furthermore, the ability for non-South Asians, who may feel excluded offline, to comfortably participate in South Asian music scenes (such as bhangra) online is noteworthy. Their presence on MySpace and Facebook not only renders visible exclusion created by South Asians offline, but also illustrates how online encounters can positively shape South Asian popular cultures offline. Durkheim (*Elementary Forms*) argued that rituals give birth to ideas of social importance. The same can be said of the online rituals of the three South Asian musical scenes I have highlighted. Their rituals and behaviors (posting on Facebook 'walls', participating in e-mail lists, posting YouTube videos, etc.) underline the possibility of online South Asian cyberspaces to function as meaningful social worlds which produce ideas of social importance online and offline (a case in point for the anti-Islamophobic leanings of the Taqwacore).

Acknowledgements

The author thanks the AHRC/ESRC 'Performance, Politics, Piety' workshop participants for their useful comments on my research and Nyle Usmani, my research assistant, who was integral to this project. Fieldwork conducted for this research was funded by a Bowdoin College faculty development grant.

Notes

1. See <http://www.myspace.com>
2. Basu 'Mantras'; Desai *Beyond Bollywood*; Dudrah 163–81; Juluri 'Music Television'; Juluri 'Global Audience'; Thomas *Imagi-Nations*.
3. Ananda Mitra 'Nations and the Internet'; 'Virtual Commonality'; 'Diasporic Web Sites'; 'Marginal Voices in Cyberspace'; 'Voices of the Marginalized on the Internet'; 'Creating Immigrant Identities in Cybernetic Space'.
4. Lal 137–72; Rai 31–57; Gopal 213–32; Gajjala *Cyber Selves*.
5. <http://cdbaby.com/cd/kominas> 15 Sept. 2008.
6. My current research on Taqwacore was conducted from September 2008 to August 2009.
7. Peer-to-peer file sharing (also known as P2P) enables individual users to share files (audio, video, and otherwise) with other interested users. Software clients such as BitTorrent and Soulseek are often used for this sharing.
8. <http://punkistani.livejournal.com/> 14 Sept. 2008.
9. <http://taqwacore.forum2u.org/> 12 Sept. 2008.

10. The back cover of their CD states: 'Copying & duplicating this album is encouraged'.
11. A view confirmed by posters at the popular alternative South Asian website Sepia Mutiny. See <http://www.sepiamutiny.com/sepia/archives/003285.html#comments> 15 Sept. 2008.
12. <http://autonomedia.org/taqwa_censorship> 10 Sept. 2008.
13. Or as Sena Hussain (qtd. in Butt 10) of the Taqwacore band Secret Trial Five puts it, 'There's so much animosity towards Muslims'.
14. Gottschalk and Greenberg *Islamophobia*; Kaplan 'Islamophobia in America'; Semati 'Culture, Difference'; Sirin and Fine 151–63. See Saeed (443–62) for a discussion of similar processes in the UK and Gardner, Karakaolus and Luchtenberg 119–36 in reference to Germany and Australia.
15. Dyson *Release 2.0*; Gates, Myhrvold and Rinerason *The Road Ahead*; and Negroponte *Being Digital*.
16. Chopra (187–206) unpacks this further, arguing that an online South Asian 'global primordiality' has developed which even permeates subaltern cyberspaces such as the online Dalit discourse.
17. E-mail interview with Basim Usmani. 28 Sept. 2008.
18. <http://www.youtube.com/watch?v=2Jz4vwPjzHU> 11 Sept. 2008.
19. E-mail interview with Basim Usmani. 28 Sept. 2008.
20. Murthy 'A South Asian American Diasporic Aesthetic Community?'; 'Communicative Flows between the Diaspora and "Homeland"'; 'Representing South Asian Alterity?'
21. <http://www.youtube.com/watch?v=gx-NLPH8JeM>.
22. Taken from The Offspring's 1998 track of the same name.
23. The 'Basement Bhangra' nights run in downtown Manhattan by DJ Rekha were an exception. The progressive politics of the nights attracted non-Asians from activist, GLBTQ, and journalistic circles.
24. In my research on Asian electronic music online, I have come across several non-Asian respondents who first participated in the scene online, making friends and building a solid knowledge and connection to the scene before participating in it offline. Speaking with them; it is clear that these initial online incursions made for a richer, more comfortable experience off-line. For example, I met John, a black British respondent with ancestry traced to Martinique, at an Asian electronic music event in Shoreditch, East London in 2006. At this club night, he recounted to me how he first participated online for several months before attending an Asian electronic music club night. Before participating online, John felt that this scene was ethnically endogamous. His online interactions with other participants of the scene challenged this notion and were a pivotal reason for his decision to participate physically in the Asian electronic music scene.
25. DJ Nerm during the 7 September 2008 Electro East radio show on BBC Asian Network.
26. From May to August 2008, I examined the MySpace pages of biracial and non-Asian bhangra fans.
27. 'White boys'.
28. These have been anonymized.
29. E-mail interview with Basim Usmani. 28 Sept. 2008.
30. For example, Karim; Gajjala; Mitra 'Marginal Voices'; Mitra 'Voices of the Marginalized'; Purkayastha *Negotiating Ethnicity*.
31. E-mail interview with Basim Usmani. 28 Sept. 2008.
32. See Lange (1–7) for a further discussion of this demonization in praxis.
33. The two main e-mail lists she studied were 'women-writing-culture' and 'SAWnet'.

Notes on contributor

Dhiraj Murthy is Assistant Professor of Sociology, Department of Sociology and Anthropology, Bowdoin College, USA. He has published on transnational diasporas, new media technologies, and critical ethnography in journals such as *Sociology*, *Ethnicities*, and the *European Journal of Cultural Studies*.

References

Adams, P.C., and R. Ghose. "India.Com: The Construction of a Space Between." *Progress in Human Geography* 27.4 (2003): 414–37. Print.

Appadurai, Arjun. *Modernity at Large: Cultural Dimensions of Globalization*. Minneapolis, London: U of Minnesota P, 1996. Print.

Banerjea, K. "Sounds of Whose Underground? The Fine Tuning of Diaspora in an Age of Mechanical Reproduction." *Theory, Culture & Society* 17 (2000): 64–79. Print.

Barsky, E. and M. Purdon. "Introducing Web 2.0: Social Networking and Social Bookmarking for Health Librarians."*Journal of the Canadian Health Library Association* 27 (2006): 65–7. Print.

Basu, Anustup. "Mantras of the Metropole: Geo-Televisuality and Contemporary Indian Cinema." Diss. U of Pittsburgh, 2005. Print.

Bhatt, C., and P. Mukta. "Hindutva in the West: Mapping the Antinomies of Diaspora Nationalism." *Ethnic and Racial Studies* 23.3 (2000): 407–41. Print.

Butt, Riazat. "Islamic Street Preachers." *The Guardian* 28 Apr. 2007. Sec. Culture. Print.

Chopra, Rohit. "Global Primordialities: Virtual Identity Politics in Online Hindutva and Online Dalit Discourse." *New Media Society* 8.2 (2006): 187–206. Print.

Crafts, Lydia. "Muhammad Rocked the Casbah: San Antonio's Muslim Punk Scene Goes National, and Europe Is Next." *The Texas Observer* 14 Dec. 2007. Web. <http://www.texasobserver.org/archives/item/15252-2653-muhammed-rocked-the-casbah-san-antonios-muslim-punk-scene-goes-national-and-europe-is-next>.

Desai, Jigna. *Beyond Bollywood: The Cultural Politics of South Asian Diasporic Film*. New York, London: Routledge, 2004. Print.

Dudrah, R.K. "Zee TV-Europe and the Construction of a Pan-European South Asian Identity." *Contemporary South Asia* 11.2 (2002): 163–81. Print.

Durkheim, Emile. *The Elementary Forms of the Religious Life: A Study in Religious Sociology*. New York: Allen and Unwin, 1926. Print.

Dyson, Esther. *Release 2.0: A Design for Living in the Digital Age*. 1st ed. New York: Broadway Books, 1997. Print.

Ellison, Nicole B., Charles Steinfield, and Cliff Lampe. "The Benefits of Facebook 'Friends': Social Capital and College Students' Use of Online Social Network Sites." *Journal of Computer-Mediated Communication* 12.4 (2007): 1143–68. Print.

Gajjala, Radhika. *Cyber Selves: Feminist Ethnographies of South Asian Women*. Lanham, MD: AltaMira, 2004. Print.

Gardner, Rod, Yasemin Karakaolus, and Sigrid Luchtenberg. "Islamophobia in the Media: A Response from Multicultural Education." *Intercultural Education* 19.2 (2008): 119–36. Print.

Gates, Bill, Nathan Myhrvold, and Peter Rinearson. *The Road Ahead*. London: Viking, 1995. Print.

Gopal, Sangita. "Home Pages: Immigrant Subjectivity in Cyberspace." *Globalization and the Humanities*. Ed. David Leiwei Li. Hong Kong: Hong Kong UP, 2004. 213–32 Print.

Gottschalk, Peter, and Gabriel Greenberg. *Islamophobia: Making Muslims the Enemy*. Lanham, Plymouth: Rowman & Littlefield Publishers, 2008. Print.

Harp, D., and M. Tremayne. "The Gendered Blogosphere: Examining Inequality Using Network and Feminist Theory." *Journalism & Mass Communication Quarterly* 83.2 (2006): 247–64. Print.

Juluri, Vamsee. *Becoming a Global Audience: Longing and Belonging in Indian Music Television*. New York: Peter Lang, 2003. Print.

Juluri, Vamsee. "Music Television and the Invention of Youth Culture in India." *Television & New Media* 3.4 (2002): 367–86. Print.

Kaplan, Jeffrey. "Islamophobia in America?: September 11 and Islamophobic Hate Crime." *Terrorism and Political Violence* 18.1 (2006): 1–33. Print.

Karim, K.H. *From Ethnic Media to Global Media: Transnational Communication Networks among Diasporic Communities*. Ottawa: Strategic Research and Analysis Directorate, Department of Canadian Heritage, 1998. Print.

Knight, Michael Muhammad. *The Taqwacores*. London: Telegram, 2007. Print.

Lal, V. "The Politics of History on the Internet: Cyber-Diasporic Hinduism and the North American Hindu Diaspora." *Diaspora* 8.2 (1999): 137–72. Print.

Lange, Werner. "Faith in Inaction: A Christian Critique of Islamophobia." *Journal of Religion and Society* 9 (2007): 1–7. Print.

Mandaville, Peter. "Communication and Diasporic Islam: A Virtual Ummah?" *The Media of Diaspora*. Ed. Karim H. Karim. London: Routledge, 2003. 135–47. Print.

Mitra, A. "Creating Immigrant Identities in Cybernetic Space: Examples from a Non-Resident Indian Website." *Media, Culture & Society* 27.3 (2005): 371–90. Print.

Mitra, A. "Diasporic Web Sites: Ingroup and Outgroup Discourse." *Critical Studies in Mass Communication* 14.2 (1997): 151–8. Print.

Mitra, A. "Marginal Voices in Cyberspace." *New Media & Society* 3.1 (2001): 29–48. Print.

Mitra, A. "Nations and the Internet: The Case of a National Newsgroup, 'Soc. Cult. Indian'." *Convergence: The International Journal of Research into New Media Technologies* 2.1 (1996): 44–75. Print.

Mitra, A. "Virtual Commonality: Looking for India on the Internet." *Virtual Culture: Identity and Communication in Cybersociety*. Ed. Steven G. Jones. Thousand Oaks, CA: Sage Publications Inc, 1997. 55–79 Print.

Mitra, A. "Voices of the Marginalized on the Internet: Examples from a Website for Women of South Asia." *Journal of Communication* 54.3 (2004): 492–510. Print.

Murthy, Dhiraj. "Communicative Flows between the Diaspora and 'Homeland': The Case of Asian Electronic Music in Delhi." *Journal of Creative Communication* 2 (2007): 143–61. Print.

Murthy, Dhiraj. "Digital Ethnography: An Examination of the Use of New Technologies for Social Research." *Sociology* 42.5 (2008): 837–55. Print.

Murthy, Dhiraj. "Representing South Asian Alterity? East London's Asian Electronic Music Scene and the Articulation of Globally Mediated Identities." *European Journal of Cultural Studies* 12.3 (2009): 329–48. Print.

Murthy, Dhiraj. "A South Asian American Diasporic Aesthetic Community? Ethnicity and New York City's 'Asian Electronic Music' Scene." *Ethnicities* 7.2 (2007): 225–47. Print.

Negroponte, Nicholas. *Being Digital*. London: Hodder & Stoughton, 1995. Print.

Purkayastha, Bandana. *Negotiating Ethnicity: Second-Generation South Asian Americans Traverse a Transnational World*. Piscataway, NJ: Rutgers UP, 2005. Print.

Rai, Amit S. "India on-Line: Electronic Bulletin Boards and the Construction of a Diasporic Hindu Identity." *Diaspora* 4.1 (1995): 31–57. Print.

Saeed, Amir. "Media, Racism and Islamophobia: The Representation of Islam and Muslims in the Media." *Sociology Compass* 1.2 (2007): 443–62. Print.

Semati, Mehdi. "Culture, Difference, and Islamophobia in the Age of the Global." Annual Meeting of the International Communication Association. San Francisco, CA. 23 May 2007. Conference Paper. <http://www.allacademic.com/meta/p173307_index.html>.

Sharma, Sanjay. "Noisy Asians or 'Asian Noise'?". *Dis-Orienting Rhythms: The Politics of the New Asian Dance Music*. Ed. Sanjay Sharma, John Hutnyk and Ashwani Sharma. London: Zed Books, 1996. 32–60 Print.

Sirin, Selcuk R., and Michelle Fine. "Hyphenated Selves: Muslim American Youth Negotiating Identities on the Fault Lines of Global Conflict." *Applied Developmental Science* 11.3 (2007): 151–63. Print.

Thomas, Amos Owen. *Imagi-Nations and Borderless Television: Media, Culture and Politics across Asia*. New Delhi; London: Sage, 2005. Print.

'Through A Lens Starkly': An exploration of JU Medialab's National Instruments Project archive

Anustup Basu

> However, with our purposeful activity, and even more, our purposeful remembering, each day unravels the web, the ornaments of forgetting. Walter Benjamin

Prologue

National Instruments Limited was an Indian public sector company located in Jadavpur, a locality toward the southern end of the city of Kolkata (formerly Calcutta). It was engaged in the design, development, and manufacture of fine opto-mechanical and opto-electronic instruments for a variety of end-users, especially those tasking in geological surveys, meteorology, and defense. The institution traced its origins to 1830, when Sir George Everest (1790–1866), the Surveyor General of India, felt the necessity of having skilled mechanical help in Calcutta itself for servicing equipment. A workshop called Mathematical Instruments Office was set up in the Dalhousie area in the central part of the city, with Syed Meer Mohsin Hussain being appointed as the first Indian master maker of fine optical and precision devices after the departure of Henry Barrow.[1] The legend, therefore, with whatever remoteness or intimacy, grafts itself into a pioneering moment of modern rational-scientific inquiry in colonial India that would include, amongst myriad things, the great trigonometric survey of the subcontinent, the mathematical achievements of Radhanath Sikdar (1813–1870), and the long shadow of the greatest mountain in the world.[2] Following that of course, the story ties up with another narrative of becoming – a non-aligned Nehruvian journey of the free Indian republic toward technological, scientific, and industrial self-sufficiency. National Instruments Ltd., in its final incarnation, moved to its location in Jadavpur in 1957, under the auspices of the second five-year plan. At its peak, the spacious premises, covering about ten acres of land, hummed with the activity of about two thousand workers.

National Instruments entered its twilight in the late eighties, reportedly because the Indian Army, for which it manufactured a range of products like infra-red search lights, passive binoculars, and night vision optical devices, gave away lucrative contracts to a Swedish company. In 1992 it was registered as a sick industry with the Board for Industrial and Financial Reconstruction (BIFR). The rate of decline was precipitous throughout the early globalizing years of the nineties, with the company steadily shedding workforce through the Indian government's Voluntary Retirement Scheme (VRS), after a rehabilitation scheme was authorized by the BIFR in 1999. Production finally halted in 2003. A year before that, in July 2002, the Department of Disinvestment in the Ministry of Finance, Government of India, announced intentions to induct a joint venture partner for NIL and called for bids, declaring that the authorized and paid-up capital of the company was INR 100 million and Rs. 83.1 million respectively.[3] Evidently such efforts did not work out. However, perhaps because of its PSU status, NIL did not meet the fate of similar old world Industrial enterprises in the vicinity, which became prime real estate.[4] Finally, in 2009, Jadavpur University absorbed the 64 remaining employees of NIL and acquired the factory site to set up a new campus there. It was in the summer of that year that I visited the NIL premises with Moinak Biswas, a friend, mentor, and an extraordinary scholar of Indian cinema and culture. That was a crucial moment, for it was in the middle of a short interregnum before the JU administration began renovating the space and exorcising ghosts to make a campus out of the factory building. Biswas, who was the Head of the JU Film Studies Department and coordinator of the university's newly formed media lab, instigated a collaborative multi-media project in which several past and present students and affiliates of the institution took part. The six month long effort yielded a remarkable artistic archive of the ephemeral, including four short films, many projects in still photography and photo animation, and one sound installation.[5]

My own recollection of the factory – derelict, dirty, spooky, and majestic – is not pertinent to this discussion. It is sufficient to say that I found the place and its surroundings poignant, haunting, intensely dramatic, and traced by an unforgiving violence of time. It was, in itself, an installation of deathly art – a monument of dusty and frozen chaos in which the ironic and the tragic folded into each other or slipped into grotesque humor. Walking through the hallways and the rooms was a wholesome synesthetic experience, with sensory surprises at every turn. The building turned especially sonorous when it rained heavily on one of the three days I was there. The sheets of water drummed in through the many broken panes of the large and numerous windows and skylights; the wind howled, resonating against the high ceilings.

It was about a year later that I saw the archive. Let me first provide a working descriptive of this astonishing body of work. Following that, the essay will turn towards a meditation on what such images and sounds could mean in our age of information and instant commodification. Do they report some sort of 'truth' in the heart of the matter, or do they problematize dominant notions of *veritas* and the image in and of themselves, especially since we never stop alerting ourselves about a long rumble of the postmodern? Do these pictures and echographies challenge already there, consumable and eminently advertisable global structures of feeling (the nostalgia industry, the memory industry, exoticism, ethnography, or orientalism), or are they subsumed by them? Do they give us an 'image' of the factory, or can they bring to fresh crisis ontological understandings of the image itself? How do they set up a relationship between art and reportage? What could be the status of this archive in relation to massified structures of statist and corporatist archiving? When it comes to vanishings and presences of forms of life in the factory, who is it that ultimately holds the name-giving powers? Who tells us when to feel wistful, when to mourn, or when to laugh heartily? Is the image that which represents, speaks volubly, or, as Rancière said, is it that which holds its tongue?[6] Let us keep these queries pending for the moment and first visit the archive.

The archive

The archive of course is made up of a number of individual projects. Each of these is distinctive on its own and deserves to be valued and recognized as such. However, after describing them briefly, I shall critically consider the archive as a singular entity when it comes to the question of the image. Let us begin with the films. Sambit Bose's short *Ekti Karkhanar Itikatha/The Story of a Factory* documents the history of NIL, using testimonies of past workers, evocative tracking of spaces, and a survey of the panoply of old, dusty instruments. Kartik Pal, the senior clerk, talks sadly about crucial errors in management policy, falling profits, losing key R&D personnel to the private sector when the winds of change drifted in with liberalization. Gautam Sarkar, technical worker,

Figure 1. NIL: The machine shop
Photo courtesy of Jadavpur University Media Lab, Madhuban Mitra, and Manas Bhattacharya

proudly displays the achievements of the past – the stereoscopic prisms, the theodolites, the passive binoculars. Mukunda Das from the Accounts section speaks about the theatrical exploits of the National Instruments Friends Club. Their last production was Girish Ghosh's Molière inspired legendary play *Jaisa Ke Taisa* in 1993. One of the remarkable aspects of Bose's film is how it connects spaces and articulated memories with unsentimental candor: the worker recreation room, the subsidized canteen that provided fifty-paisa meals, the machine shop filled with ghostly structures, and the overlooking second floor windows from which the officers could get a panoptic, monitoring perspective of the workers down below. The camera cuts away frequently from these testimonies – sometimes fond, sometimes sad – to track and linger around the dusty and forlorn spaces in which a thousand human voices have been lost.

Ankur Das's *Graveyard of Memories* is a more forensic exploration of space. The factory is more cadaverous and elemental here; the camera works like a scalpel, extracting abstract patterns of matter and movement, often through the judicious use of extreme close-ups. It tracks corruption and break-outs of colors, worn down textures, inscriptions of moisture, wind, rust, putrefaction, and decay. The sheen of finely finished glass is seen to be rendered iridescent and then buried by dust; different clocks are frozen at different points in time; empty chairs occupy emptiness. This graveyard of memories is intensely naturalistic; it is one in which vegetation creeps and roots into cracks of devastated concrete and spiders weave their webs in between objects, inventing a primordial clutter by tying things together and exiling them from their social histories. Out-of-frame sounds (sirens, telephones, rain, machines) of a busy diurnal world are exhausted when they are juxtaposed with the deathly stillness of the premises. The film presents inertia as a durational intensity through loop montages that break and then come together once again with slow, elegiac maturation. Das's film shares an experimental spirit of exploring dead space as enervated and thick time with *Underneath the Sky of Rust*, a short workshop film made by 'Group A'[7] of the Jadavpur University Film Studies Department students. The latter work distinguishes itself especially with a few slow zooms, and a haunting sound track featuring abrupt conversations and strains from from Pink Floyd ('Welcome to the Machine' and 'Echoes'). A former unnamed employee responds to questions we do not hear, sitting on a chair in the middle of a grime covered floor on which, once upon a time, no shoes or foreign particles were allowed. Searching camera movements underline the fact that once processes of serialization, electrification, and production have ceased, there is no particular direction one can go inside the factory, since objects, having lost their destinies and lineages, are no longer useful in signposting and mapping. They simply occupy a ground, often not revealing whether it is by design or accident. The factory, in both *Graveyard* and *Sky of Rust*, is dirt in the heart of the city. The factory is dirt because it is now matter out of historical space and historical time.

Sanjeet Chowdhury's *Letters to Mother* is an imaginative account of an anonymous young worker's epistolary reports of his life in the factory, written between 4 February and 6 October, 1980. The letters are recited as a continuous voice-over, with the camera making random movements across derelict zones and scanning decrepit objects in black and white. Chowdhury heightens the irony by saturating the soundscape with a spectrum of noises (telephones, machines, voices, traffic, sirens, typewriters, a beating heart, and even warfare between Romans and revolting slaves) and animating the inert mise-en-scène with rapid on-shoulder pans, tracking movements and blue holographic digital diagrams. The narrative begins with the young man writing excitedly about his new workplace and its impressive heritage. It then moves to simple thrills of being served fish three times in the canteen, robust activity inside the machine shop and the paint shop, and a word of praise from his supervisor. Our protagonist talks about his new friendship with Gautam, a colleague in the optical department and his neighbour. He is soon promoted to a desk job upstairs after four months. He describes some of the products with obvious pride, but also admits the tedium of regimented labor – as his colleague from the machine shop once said, punch cards are like chains on the feet of workers. In between the young man falls sick, but is nursed back to health by Gautam's young sister Tuni, who is appearing for her school final examinations. He also joins the Worker's Union, and preparations begin for the staging of Badal Sircar's 1972 play *Spartacus* to commemorate the union's 25th anniversary. The play would eventually be staged on 26 March, 1981. The story however ends before that, with our young man writing to his mother on 6 October, 1980, saying that he would be coming home for the Pujas and that he would be bringing good news with him.

The volume of still photographs by Madhuban Mitra, Manas Bhattacharya, Nikhil Arolkar, and the distinguished cinematographer Abheek Mukhopadhyay is equally remarkable, as is the sound installation *Frozen Noise* by Sukanta Majumdar. Mitra and Bhattacharya have organized their work into an exhibit entitled 'Through a Lens Darkly' that has been, in the last two years, exhibited in Singapore, Greece, the Netherlands, the United Kingdom, and Hungary, apart from several cities in India. Here the still images are ordered into a few component sections and are accompanied by four photo animations made 'by clicking a lot of pictures at a high speed and then merging them to show light and wind playing visual illusions on the broken assembly tables'.[8] 'The Archaeology of Absence' is a series that offers glimpses of a range of private quiddities (a shirt hung up and left behind as if for eternity) in the factory; 'Persistent Circuits' traces geometrical patterns on walls, wires, and switchboards; 'Temp Mort' features clocks that have stopped and 'Post Datum' shelves and shelves of documents and files now at the mercy of insects

Figure 2. The National Reflex 2000 model placed in the lobby
Photo courtesy of Jadavpur University Media Lab, Madhuban Mitra, and Manas Bhattacharya

and the elements. 'Autopsy of the Great Indian Camera' features the dissected skeletal components of NI's most iconic product, the National 35 Sprinty BC still camera that was made in the late seventies by licensing the design of and then reverse engineering the then obsolete German product Regula Sprinty BC. There were, in all, five models of the National 35, including two pocket-size versions. One of the most resonant motifs featured regularly in the various undertakings of the National Instruments Project is the huge model of the National Reflex 2000 in the lobby of the main building, a product that was being developed when the factory closed down. It would have been India's first indigenously manufactured SLR camera.

The image in the archive

Let me begin this section by stating what, by now, could be an obvious point: since we have long since climbed down from the high horses of aesthetic modernism, I am trying to make a working distinction between picture/sound and image, following a spirit of inquiry pursued by Rancière (who we have already recalled) in his meditations on the image as a non-realistic, non-naturalistic entity that produces dissemblance by not being exclusive to the visible, and earlier, by Benjamin in his conceptualization of the dialectical image, Adorno in his aesthetics of contradiction, and Lyotard in his work on the sublime. All pictures are not images; too many of them condemn things to end up in the deserts of advertising or information. We therefore turn to a question we have suspended for a while. It pertains to a possible ontology of the image. That is, the image not taken in a commonplace, positive sense (for it seems no longer possible to do so), but as a figure of thought. Is there an image of the factory as ruin in the manifold pictures contained in the archive? That is, when we consider the image as a singular figural instance of that which is not beholden to the merely phenomenological, but a non-numbering One that in itself opens up a multiplicity. We would like to ask: is there an image of the factory in the archive?

This merits consideration because pictures and sounds that come from acts of witnessing, documenting, or mourning are imperilled in many ways. Their social lives are tested by powerful gravitational forces of the nostalgia industry, virtual tourism, ethnography, or the information age. It is important to quickly remind ourselves of the obvious, that powerful corporations like CNN today microsource accidental visuals from quotidian cell phones and handycams in Iran or Egypt or Tunisia, enframing them into pre-existing grids of reckoning, like 'freedom' is ontologically tied to 'free market' and America is a reluctant behemoth. Pictures and sounds are also claimed by the state as the entity which, as Debord once said, tries to emerge as the Napoleonic figure to monarchically direct 'the energy of memories.'[9] They are interrogated in terms of whether they are amenable to regimes of truth (from anthropology to orientalism) that capitalize and order things. They are evaluated in terms of newsworthiness when news in our informational world, as Derrida astutely observed, is that in which 'actuality' tends to be 'spontaneously ethnocentric.'[10] Consider the images of political posters in the factory that tell us of a once vibrant tradition of left-wing trade unionism. Are they supposed to automatically consign the entire cosmology of the factory to a doleful yet knowing ethnographic diagnosis emerging from a commonsensical neoliberal understanding of West Bengal's long dalliance with Marxist politics, an endemic lack of 'work culture,' 'militant trade unionism,' and the consequent flight of capital from that state? A dominant template of 'news' has to instantly induct words and images into a closed web of associations that in turn can be submitted to axiomatic narratives and dominant myths of our times – the Nehruvian past, the neoliberalism of the present at the end of history or in the middle of a war of civilizations.

The critical task is of course not to imagine that the archive, in its social existence, can be, or even should be, 'protected' from such powerful, industrial ecologies of affect, remembrance, narration, and meaning. No production is possible with such willful exile. The purpose instead is to forge a stance of textualization devoted to alterity; it is not to fondly mourn a monument or the end of a narrative, but to present a counter memory. The task therefore is not to argue whether some of the pictures provide authentic representation or whether the odd one lapses into exoticism. Rather it is to liberate them from phenomenological burdens of 'truth,' 'authenticity' and 'representation,' and also, without dodging the question of exoticism for instance, to gauge to what extent such pictures and sounds insert themselves into an overall informatic ecology of exoticism in a manner that announces the exotic itself as what Benjamin would perhaps call an 'ornament of forgetting.'[11] The thought of the image is thus the thought of trapping things in a double bind, folding its positive status as pure object with its inevitable epistemologico-industrial one of spectacle, phenomenon, or curiosity. The factory is in ruins. The ruins are a historical landscape of signs assuming the shape of a factory.

We will, therefore, draw imaginative powers from the archive and *textualize*, keeping in mind that the Latin *textus* means web, being the perfect passive participle of *texō*, which means 'to weave.' Let us turn to the scattered visuals of the 'private' that we find: a love letter, a pack of cards, a mosquito repellent sprayer, a whiskey bottle, a box of chewing tobacco (*Baba Kesari Zarda*), a tin of Colgate tooth powder, a pair of slippers eternally waiting for footsteps, medicines, clothing on lines, images of gods and goddesses, personal idols (Indira Gandhi, Tagore), a poster featuring legendary movie stars Hema Malini and Dharmendra, an old issue of the *Soviet Literature* magazine, a tumbler, and a citation from Henrik Ibsen's *Enemy of the People* ('The strongest man in the world is he who stands alone') boldly emblazoned on a wall. The thought of the image here, let us propose, is

Figure 3. NIL: The machine shop
Photo courtesy of Jadavpur University Media Lab, Madhuban Mitra, and Manas Bhattacharya

not of these that are visible. It is that of an acutely compressed interval of time in which a sudden transformation seems to have taken place like the sudden demise of a bridge; a cleft had opened up between the factory and its world. It is as if after such an event, no return, in a historical sense, was possible and owners were permanently distanced from their sundry intimate possessions. The acute compression of time (when there was only time to go and not for coming back) was thus followed by eternal suspension. A shock, a violent striation in the temporal order had wrenched these things from sensuous belongings; following that, time seemed to have stopped flowing and congealed itself around these objects. We can align this double image of time – one that suddenly makes things orphans and then mummifies them – to a piece of graffiti inscribed on a drilling machine that announces 14 March, 2003 as the historic VRS day. That is, we can align the two without necessarily insisting on a positive connection. The historic VRS day was when 503 employees embraced the voluntary retirement option. This was in the middle of an overall decline in the factory population, when it lost hundreds of workers within a few months.[12] An employee wistfully recalls in Bose's *Ekti Karkhanar Itikatha* that the factory suddenly looked dead on the morning of 1 April, 2003. Attempting to run the show was like trying to cover a cadaver with a small piece of cloth.

Let us now turn to another set of visual attributes, the abstract, accidental patterns discovered and tracked by the various cameras: warts of moisture on the walls, ripples on water puddles, designs of rust on metal, cobwebs, creepers, roots, and lines of dirt that seem to tie things together, or maps of lost continents created by cracks and paint falling off walls. They indeed open up another unfolding universe of writing. What could be the visual significance of the remarkable, almost three minute long sequence of a spider spinning industriously in Das's *Graveyard of Memories*? What could be the status, qua the thought of the image, of the geographies of clutter – breaks, alignments, parallelisms, ruptures, displacements, centerings and de-centerings – unfolded by shifting perspectives of the camera as it surveys many things thrown together by chance or design? There are immense possibilities in the critical adjacency between the wash cloth and the machine, for they challenge name-giving powers.

These reminded me of what Benjamin had to say about the optical unconscious of photography. It would perhaps be useful to cite the passage in full:

> Photography reveals ... material physiognomic aspects, image worlds, which dwell in the smallest things – meaningful yet covert enough to find a hiding place in waking dreams, but which, enlarged and capable of formulation, make the difference between technology and magic visible as a thoroughly historical variable. Thus, Bossfeldt with his astonishing plant photographs reveals the forms of ancient columns in horse willow, a bishop's crosier in the ostrich fern, totem poles in tenfold enlargements of chestnut and maple shoots, and gothic tracery in the fuller's thistle.[13]

The question of the optical unconscious can be affiliated to an idea of the primordial that complicates the workings of narration, memory, historicity, and cognition in relation to the pictures in the archive. Is that a rotting wall or a demon inscribed on a surface by time itself? Is that a clown's head or rust on a doorknob? Are those dusty lenses on a table or a diagram of a devastated beehive? Is there a dinosaur next to the typing machine? The power of the primordial is that which unleashes the thought of the image by splintering the picture in many directions. It comes to the fore, not when an entity has just physically decayed, but when it has fallen off the dominant order of historical time, when it has been abandoned by the many propulsive themes of the latter (progress, development, economy). It is then that the geometrical patterns appear to thread together and invest things with a primordial aura (a discursive murmur that Foucault notices lining forms in spaces visited by Blanchot[14]) that comes just before they sink into the womb of time itself. The walls will be repainted and doorknobs will be coated once again in the new dispensation, but the image of a terrible beauty has already been born.

Figure 4. The National Reflex 2000 model
Photo courtesy Jadavpur University Media Lab, Madhuban Mitra, and Manas Bhattacharya

Finally, we come to the myriad 'public' elements great and small we find in the archive: stray dogs on the lobby floors, political posters, rickety furniture of various kinds, stacked files, old typewriters that can still snap inkless keys into place, calendars, stopped clocks, myriad dusty instruments, the old punch card machine, the guillotine used to cut sheets which also once claimed an operator's finger, rusty Ambassador cars with flattened tires and license plates from the sixties, or a framed snakes and ladders chart titled 'Game of Productivity.' One can add to these the tracking shots in the films across floor spaces, rooms, and corridors (when there is nowhere to go inside the factory), the long shots of the outskirts, or the tilt-ups towards the sky. Do these constitute an image of a micro-universe, even if it is a lost or tattered one? Perhaps they do, but it is also possible that the thought of the image comes to the fore when the pictures *run into* something. That is, they run into a void where there was a world that the factory, to borrow and transpose a theme from Heidegger, once had 'set itself back into,' and the world, in turn, had come forth to shelter it.[15] *That* world is gone from the pictures, so they give us an image of absolute and abject interiority without an 'outside'; time therefore is thick here and devoid of the present tense; the floor is a graveyard and the sky is full of rust; the factory is deserted because a desert has surrounded it. It is in this zone of perpetual arrest and historical detention that the archive posits as the site of the image's naissance, between past and present, between life and death, between the story of the factory and a legend as impressive as the tallest mountain in the world.

Notes

1 This story is stated in Sambit Bose's *Ekti Karkhanar Itikatha/History of a Factory* (2009), one of the films discussed in this essay. See also Partha Ghose, 'Scientific Studies in Calcutta: The Colonial Period' in Sukanta Chaudhuri ed. *Calcutta: The Living City, Volume I: The Past* (Calcutta: Oxford University Press, 1990): 195–202.
2 I am of course alluding to Sikdar's 1852 mathematical identification of Peak XV in the Great Trigonometrical Survey as the tallest mountain in the world. The peak, as we know, was named after Everest by Andrew Waugh, the then Surveyor General of India, with a characteristic colonial disregard for local names.
3 See http://www.divest.nic.in/nil.asp, accessed 15 June, 2011.
4 The premises of both the Sulekha Ink factory and Dabur Industries a few miles down southward along the Rajah Subodh Chandra Mullick Road have been transformed into apartment complexes now. The extensive compound of the Usha factory, west of NIL on Prince Anwar Shah Road, houses 'South City,' currently one of the biggest real estate complexes and malls in Eastern India.
5 A part of the archive can be accessed at the JU media lab website: http://www.medialabju.org/index.php.
6 See Jacques Rancière, *The Future of the Image*, trans. Gregory Elliott, (New York: Verso, 2009): 11.
7 The members were Agrajit Roy, Anurima Das, Rini Sarkar, Sourav Dey, Subhadra Mukhopadhyay, Utsab Sen, and Wriddhayan Bhattacharyya.
8 See the report entitled 'Still moments, forgotten factory' in *The Sunday Guardian*, December 26, 2010 http://www.sunday-guardian.com/home/still-moments-forgotten-factory.
9 Guy Debord, *Society of the Spectacle*, trans. Donald Nicholson Smith, (New York: Zone books, 1996): 76.
10 See Jacques Derrida and Bernard Stiegler, *Echographies of Television* (Cambridge, MA: Polity Press, 2002): 4.
11 Walter Benjamin, 'On the Image of Proust' in *Selected Writings, Vol. II (1927-1934)* (Cambridge, MA: Belknap, 1999): 238.
12 Initially 523 employees filed for the option on that day; twenty of them withdrew at the last moment. After 14 March, 68 employees were left, of which 4 took VRS before Jadavpur University took over in January 2009.

13 Benjamin, 'Little History of Photography' in *Selected Writings, Vol II*, 512.
14 See Michel Foucault, 'This is not a Pipe' in James D. Faubion ed. *Essential Works of Michel Foucault, Volume II: Aesthetics, Method, and Epistemology* (New York: The New Press, 1998): 187–204.
15 I am alluding to Heidegger's overall meditations in 'The Origin of the Work of Art' in *Basic Writings*, ed. David Farrell Krell, (New York: HarperSanFrancisco, 1977): 139–212.

Composite photography

Amit Rai

Department of English, Florida State University, Tallahassee, USA

These photographs seem to me to have come together quite by chance, but then they also emerged from patterns of behavior and forms of style, against the backdrop of flows of people, traffic, capital, information. In India today these patterns are emerging through a new ecology of sensation. However, I make no claim for these photographs as 'art.' Yet clearly the history of perspectivalism, the dominance of representationalism in the engagement with a living multiplicity is at stake for me in creating these images. There is an accretion of information some of which coheres, much of which does not, but each image has a certain duration at different scales of perception, a non-coinciding resonant unity, a unity-in-multiplicity is what I hope to continue through the photography (mutating affect, not representation). An ecology of sensation meeting its cliché: Bollywood meets graphic novels at the back of a rickshaw, Agra's Mughal-era oriental(ized) stone work turning topological and dimensional (is it less or more racist? To what extent is the question relevant to what it does?), the Ferris wheel on Juhu beach, the weighing machine at the local station. This time that I have been able to spend here in India, thanks to a research grant from the Fulbright foundation, has allowed me to research the materiality of the ecology of sensation of mobile phones and experiment in forms of creatively engaging this ecology.

Cinematically, I have been inspired by the work of Anurag Kashyap, the acting of Abhay Deol, the inventiveness of Gulzar and Javed Akhtar, the interpretive voice of Jagjit Singh, the clarity of Naseerudin Shah; the power of Vidya Balan; conceptually the scholarship of Nivedita Menon and Shilpa Phadke has brought me new resources for imagining justice and democracy. Gilles Deleuze's words echo in this mutating practice (specifically *What is Philosophy* and *Nietzsche and Philosophy*).

Riding out the cliché that we each singularly (and so collectively: all habits are pre-individual: where the subject and populations meet) have become is not like riding a wave, a horse, or a sexual partner. These photographs have no metaphor, but it is easy to find various metaphors in them. They have attempted to accrete digital information, to assemble, to form what artist and photographer Ranjit Khandalgoankar (and contemporary engineering) calls transient states (the work of Ranjit and James Mazza has affected me, see respectively: http://cityinflux.com/transient.html; http://alexianimages.wordpress.com/). Again not as *mise en abime* but as potential occasions for a perceptual event (events that exceed their actualization). Ranjit and I have also discussed the limitations of

Figure 1. Platform 1 and 2, Chhatrapati Shivaji Terminus, Mumbai.

Figure 2. Crores Worldwide, 'My Name is Khan' Hoarding, Juhu Beach, Mumbai.

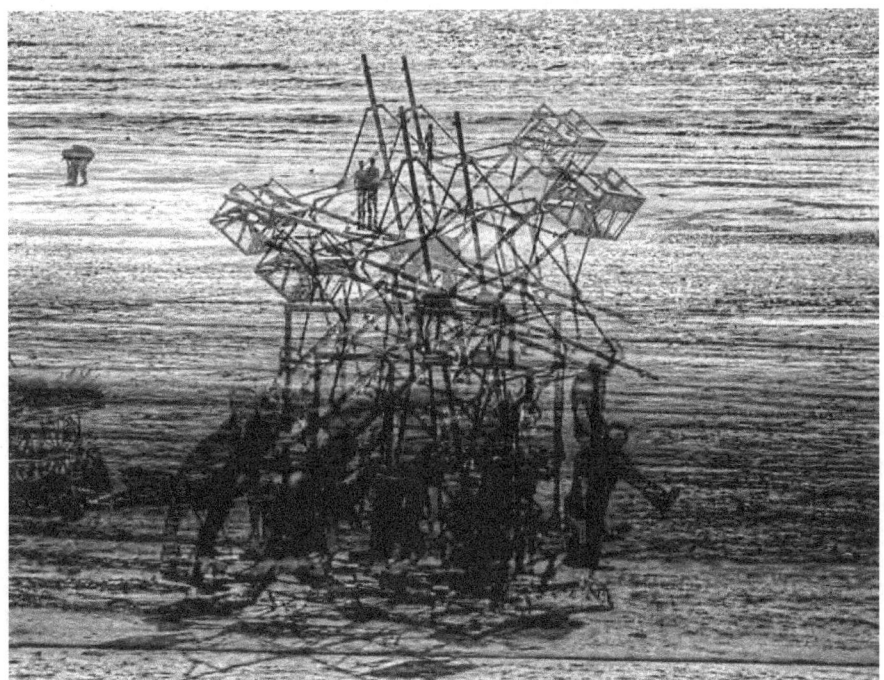

Figure 3. Workers setting up Ferris wheel, Juhu Beach, Mumbai.

Figure 4. Harbor Line to Chhatrapati Shivaji Terminus, Mumbai.

Figure 5. Traffic Signal, Kundanahali, Bangalore.

Figure 6. Abandoned Factory, Umerkhadi, Mumbai.

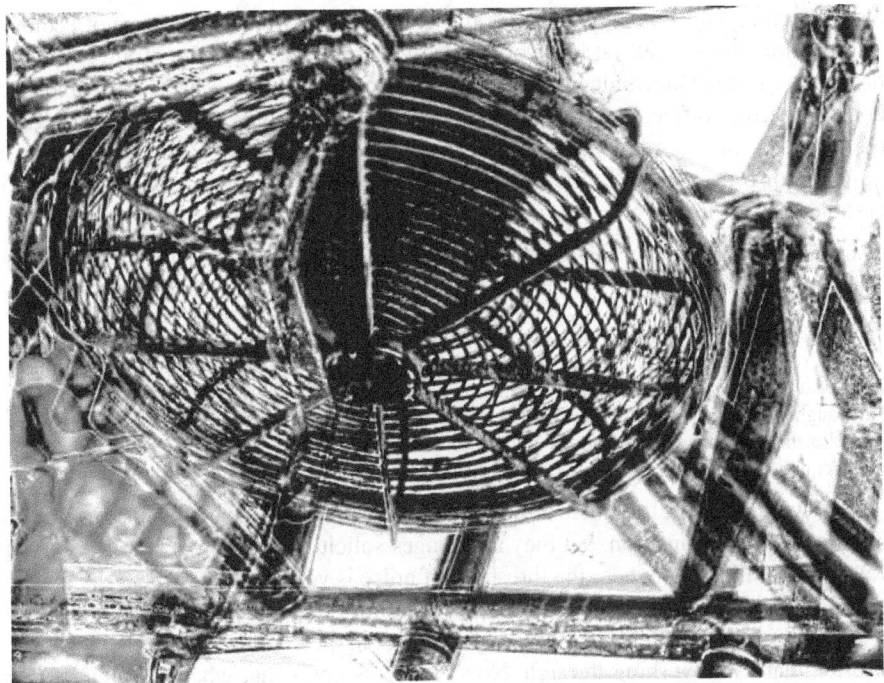

Figure 7. Hand, Fan, Local Train, Mumbai.

photography, especially as forms of ethnography or visual anthropology; photography whose photoshopped life in fact betrays the promise of photography itself; photographs that enable a hauntology to emerge in the viewing subject. These photographs do not do all that, in that respect they do very little aside from pointing the capacities of perception in multiple directions. From the very beginning of our conversation, the aim was to find forms beyond narration. His notion of transient states is crucial for precisely this reason. He is interested in switches; I am interested in the switching of bodily senses. This is not a celebration of transient life as resistance; it is an affirmation of becoming from the molecular to the molar, but always beginning against a backdrop of emergent patterns and forms, that is of relations of force, sense, and value. These photographs have solicited my vision; they strike me as potential events in gradients of textured vision, haptic and mutating across senses.

However, this is not to make too much of them. They are just my own photographs composited onto my own photographs on a readily available program called AKVIS, and different control parameters knobs – luminosity, RGB, colors, level of detail, contrast, brightness, saturation, high and low lights, and the such – tweaked until something, some sensation compels me. An excess takes hold, where one gets the sense of movement in a transient state. They are not *mise en abime*, and at their best (admittedly a rare occurrence) something resonates beyond the image, beyond the screen or page through which they are experienced and we enter a realm of excessive information that calls for another diagram of bodily capacities. The experience of making these photographs has helped me to grasp some words of Isabelle Stengers.

Stengers gives us a clear image of thought as well as forceful concept of the way difference functions in far from equilibrium systems. In fact, it is a rejection of a priori conceptualism, and opting instead for a practice of emergence. Not that the practice is constantly emerging (it is mutating), but that it is involved in the emergence of ecologies. Stengers (drawing as well on her work with Ilya Prigogine) writes of strange attractors, whose systems have an irreducible aleatory force passing through them repetitively, and whose properties (affects) vary with sudden changes in force, passing from basin of attraction to basin of attraction. Given a statistical probability of variance in a process, in a population of processes, irregular forces transform noise into the occasion of a dynamic threshold. She writes:

> Far from equilibrium, fluctuations may cease to be noise, instead becoming actors that play a role in changing the macroscopic regime of a system. Furthermore, the far-from-equilibrium physiochemical systems that Ilya Prigogine baptized 'dissipative structures' exhibit another new property. It is not only 'molecular noise,' the fluctuations, that may 'take on meaning' but also certain details of the control variables that correspond to the experimental definition of the system under study (pressure, volume, temperature, flow of reagents, ...). For example, although gravitation has no observable effect on chemical systems at equilibrium or near to equilibrium, far from equilibrium its effect can be amplified so that it has macroscopic consequences. The system has become sensitive to gravitation. (9–12)

Now we make no claim that these photographs are non-linear systems, nor do they inaugurate a phase transition, but they are images soliciting perceptual capacities tending away from equilibrium, where the threshold of noise is very low, and where the machinic phylum becomes sensitive to certain forces (of luminosity or the color blue or saturation, for instance). The photographs are experiments in perception given the ecology of sensation that I am working through. Now, Stengers notes that when a system becomes sensitive to certain forces, dynamics, processes, an emergent property comes into play in the new system. These emergent properties open the system to the machinic phylum and the nonlinear plane of potential. How? The very concept of becoming, the components of this concept – intensity, chance, mutation, sensation, value, force, sense – have a statistically apprehendable (but not determinate) variance. At critical thresholds this population of variant processes becomes sensitive to forces simultaneously, instantaneously and in that transient state a phase transition is inaugurated.

> Similiarly, it has been shown that a dissipative structure fed by chemical flows that are not perfectly constant in time but slightly irregular has access to new types of structuation. In other words, it is the collective regime of activity that decides what is insignificant noise and what must be taken into account. We do not know a priori what a chemical population can do, and we can no longer tell once and for all the difference between what we must take into account and what we can ignore .... A demon that understood and could control with positively infinite precision a system characterized by such an attractor could obviously deal with it as just another system. For the demon, the system would be deterministic, as are the equations that describe it. However, is this reference still relevant? We are not actually separated from the demon by a quantitative lack (we observe and manipulate less well) but by a qualitative difference: as long as our observations and manipulations do not have a strictly infinite precision, we are dealing with a system with nondeterministic behavior.... Here the notion of complexity is close to that of emergence. Dangerously close, moreover, if, as is often the case, 'emergence' is understood as the appearance of the unanalyzable totality of a new entity that renders irrelevant the intelligibility of that which produced it. (Stengers 9, 10, 12)

Stengers goes on to argue that the difference between emergence and complexity is that of a physical genesis in contrast to a conceptual genesis. Can concepts become involved in a machinic phylum in any other relation than one of capture and reduction? This has been the wager in these photographs. They are not representations of a philosophy, Deleuzian or otherwise. They are experimentations in framing, saturation, luminosity, perspective, topology, movement, shadow, detail, hapticity. They are not philosophy; they attempt the production of affect that resonates with a conceptual and bodily becoming.

Notes on contributor

Amit S. Rai is an associate professor of film, media, and postcolonial studies at Florida State University. He received his Ph.D. in Modern Thought and Literature from Stanford University in 1995, and has taught at the New School for Social Research and Florida State University. He is the author of *Rule of Sympathy: Race, Sentiment, and Power* (Palgrave, 2002). He has written on Indian masculinity in film, anthropologies of monstrosity, sympathetic discursive relations, and the swerves of media (*clinamedia*). His study of new media in India, entitled *Untimely Bollywood: Globalization and India's New Media Assemblage* was published by Duke University Press in 2009. His blog on the history of media assemblages and the politics of perception can be found at http://mediaecologiesresonate.wordpress.com. He is presently in India on a Fulbright Senior Research Fellowship diagramming the perceptual mutations involved in gender identity and mobile phone networks in urban areas.

References

Deleuze, Gilles. *Nietzsche and Philosophy*. Trans. Hugh Tomlinson. New York: Columbia UP, 2006. Print.
Deleuze, Gilles, and Felix Guattari. *What is Philosophy?* Trans. Hugh Tomlinson et al. New York: Columbia UP, 1996. Print.
Stengers, Isabelle. "Complexity: A Fad?" *Power and Invention*. Minneapolis: U of Minnesota P, 1997. 9–12. Print.

Index

Page numbers in **Bold** represent figures.

activism 28
actor-network theory (ANT) 3, 22
Ahmedabad International Film Festival (AIFF) 21, 25–36
Alliance Francaise 27
Althusser, L. 39–40
Anti-Sikh riots (1984) 48
Appadurai, A. 91
Asia: media market 65
assimilation 62
auto-erotism 50

Back, L.: and Nayak, A. 59
Basu, A. 101–9
Bazin, A. 23
Benjamin, W. 23, 108
Berlin Film Festival 26
Bhangra music 65–6
Bhatt, A. 81
bin Laden, O. 38
bio-political processes 41
black representation 58
Board for Industrial and Financial Reconstruction (BIFR) 101
Boltanski, L. 80
Bolter, J.D.: and Grusin, R. 8; image 12
Bose, S. 102; *Ekti Karkhanar Itikatha* 107
Brasher, B. 7
Brass, P. 77
Breder, H. 42
business models 2
Butler, J. 41

Cannes Film Festival 30
Chandra, S. 60
Chinay, A. 47
Chion, M.: *The Voice in Cinema* 52
Chow, R.: narcissism 40; *The Protestant Ethnic and the Spirit of Capitalism* 39
Chowdhury, S.: *Letters to Mother* 104
Christianity 77
Cinefan Film Festival 26

cinema: development 32; independent 29; India 24; international 20
communal discourse 81
communalism 71
communication networks 14
community 16, 61–2
consumer goods 64
crisis 82
cultural resource 51
culturalist movements 91
cyberspace 7
Cybertaqwa 90

Das, A.: *Graveyard of Memories* 103
Das, M. 103
Dastoor, C. 25
Dayan, D. 19
De Valck, M. 24; *Film Festivals* 22
deities 6–17
Department of Philosophy and Religious Studies 8
diaspora 15; autobiography 39–42
diasporic identities 62–4
diasporic mediascapes 58
digital darshan 11
Dolphin Media Group 60
Dudrah, R. 58–66

Eck, D.L 10
economic liberalization 70
Ekti Karkhanar Itikatha (Bose) 107
Elsaesser, T. 20
Enemy of the People (Ibsen) 106
ethical redefinition 53
ethnic narcissism 41
Euro Zindagi (TV programme) 61
European identity 58–9, 64
Everest, G. 101

Facebook 96–7
faith communities 7
film festivals 19–36; cultural logic 24–5
Film Festivals (De Valck) 22

INDEX

Flaherty Film Seminar 32
Fletcher, J. 53
forums 32
Foucault, M. 22
Freccero, C. 50
Freud, S. 39; *On Narcissism* 45
Fung, R. 47

Gandhi, R. 72
Ganesh Temples 10
gender 12, 92
genocide 78
Gill, H.: queer intermediation 49
global recession 15
global warming 33
Goa Film Festival 26
Gopal, S. 13
Graveyard of Memories (Das) 103
Green, A. 45
Grusin, R.: and Bolter, J.D. 8; image 12
Gujarat carnage (2002) 70–83

Hindu Right movements 79
Hinduism 9; worship traditions 11
Hindutva masculinity 92
homophobia 49
homosexualization 39
human-divine interactions 9
Hunter, A. 52
hypertextual links 16
hysteria 38

Ibsen, H.: *Enemy of the People* 106
identification 49
identity 45, 60–1
incommensurability 53
independent cinema 29
Independent Film Bazaar 21
India: cinema 24; film festivals 19–36; masculinity 47; media culture 76
Indian Directorate of Film Festivals 23
Indian Institute of Management (IIM) 27
Indian Partition (1947) 48
Indianization 16
Indo-German Association 62
interactivity 13
intermedia: in diaspora 38–53; ecologies 2; performance 52–3
international cinema 20
International Film Festival of India (IFFI) 20
International Initiative for Justice (IIJ) 78
Iowa State University 8

Jadavpur University 104
Jagose, A. 51
Jain, A. 70–83
Jaitley, A. 75

JU Medialab 101–9

Kerala Film Festival 29
Khan, S.R. 31
Khandalgoankar, R. 111
Klemm, D.E. 42
Knight, M.M. 88

Laplanche, J. 45
Latour, B. 22
LeCarré, J. 38
Letters to Mother (Chowdhury) 104

Magic Lantern Foundation 20
mainstream culture 27
Maitra, A. 38–53
Mallapragada, M. 6–17
manipulation thesis 72
marginalization 40
masculinity 47
media 59; cultures 7, 15; debates 71–3; ecology 1; networks 14; organizations 74; ownership 70; representatives 73
melancholia 38
Milind Soman Made Me Gay (Singh) 3, 42–50
mimeticism 40
Mitra, A. 91
Mitra, C. 75
Modi, N. 71
moral responsibility 81
Munich Film Festival 33
Muñoz, J.E. 42
Murdoch, R. 60
Murthy, D. 87–97

narcissism: transindividual 41
The Nation (magazine) 38
National Institute of Design (NID) 27
National Instruments Friends Club 103
National Instruments Ltd. 4
National Instruments Project 101–9
National Reflex model **105**
nationalism 28
Nayak, A.: and Back, L. 59
neoliberalism 2
News Corporation Ltd 60
Noble Drew (band) 93, **95**

Ojha, K. 35
O'Leary, S. 7
On Narcissism (Freud) 45
ostracization 80

Parekh, B. 79
perspectivalism 111
photography 111–16

INDEX

Pioneer (newspaper) 75
popular culture 1
Prasad, M. 19
Prashad, V. 12
The Protestant Ethnic and the Spirit of Capitalism (Chow) 39
psychic identification 46

queer pedagogy 51

Rai, A. 111–16
Rajadhyaksha, A. 19
Rajagopal, A. 76
Ram Janmabhumi movement 75
Rangan, P. 19–36
Regula Sprinty BC 105
religion 77
remediation 8
representation 4; forms 16
repression 40
rituals 8

Sabha, R. 82
Sarkar, G. 102–3
Scheifinger, H. 14
Sedgwick, E.K. 41
September 11th 73
sexual marginalization 49
Shamiana Short Film Club 25
Sibal, K. 82
Siddiqui, S. 82
Sikdar, R. 101
Singh, A. 21, 25–36
Singh, H.: *Milind Soman Made Me Gay* 3, 42–50
Singhal, A. 79
Sircar, B.: *Spartacus* 104
Smith, Z.: *White Teeth* 59
social media 90
social networking 94
society 33
socio-political culture 72
Soman, M. 44
South Asia: community 61; identities 91–3; popular culture 93–4

Spartacus (Sircar) 104
Spivak, G.C. 50
Star News 74
Stengers, I. 115
subculture 87–97

Taqwacore (music movement) 88–91
technologies 82
temple spaces 13
Time (magazine) 6
time-space relations 13
trade unionism 106
transindividualism 50
transnational spaces 4
transnationalization 93
Tulli, N. 31

value-added services (VAS) 1
Vasudevan, R. 23
victimization 78
Virtual Reality Applications Center 8
Vishwa Hindu Parishad (VHP) 71
The Voice in Cinema (Chion) 52
Voluntary Retirement Scheme (VRS) 101

Wenner, D. 35
Western public culture 90
White Teeth (Smith) 59
Wide Angle 26
work culture 106
Worker's Union 104
World Trade Centre 73
worship 10

Your Zindagi (TV programme) 61

Zee TV 58–66

www.routledge.com/9780415698450

Related titles from Routledge

South Asian Cinemas

Widening the Lens

Edited by Sara Dickey and Rajinder Dudrah

This path-breaking collection explores the breadth and depth of South Asia's many vibrant cinemas. It extends well beyond Bollywood to Nepali, Sri Lankan, Pakistani Panjabi, Bhojpuri, Bengali, Kannada, and early Tamil cinemas, while unpacking the category of 'Bollywood' itself. The coverage of cinematic features is equally far-ranging, exploring music, dance, audiences, filmmakers, industries, and the mutual influences among South Asia's cinemas.

With a mix of ethnographic, historical, auteur, and textual approaches, this exciting collection presents the first wide-reaching analysis of South Asian cinemas, and will be novel reading for a new generation of work into an important global cinematic region.

This book was originally published as a special issue of *South Asian Popular Culture*.

November 2011: 246 x 174: 152pp
Hb: 978-0-415-69845-0
£80 / $125

For more information and to order a copy visit
www.routledge.com/9780415698450

Available from all good bookshops